I CAN'T TAKE BACK My Yes

MICHELE
DECAUL

I Can't Take Back My Yes: Emerging with Victory through Cancer, Death, and Grief by Michele DeCaul
Published by Michele DeCaul/The DeCaul Foundation
522 Hunt Club Blvd., Suite 139
Apopka, Fl. 32703
www.micheledecaul.com
www.thedecaulfoundation.net

Visit the author's website at www.micheledecaul.com

International Standard Book Number: 979-8-9926812-0-8

While the author has made every effort to provide accurate internet addresses at the time of publication, neither the publisher nor the author assumes any responsibility for errors or for changes that occur after publication. Further, the publisher does not have any control over and does not assume any responsibility for author or third-party websites or their content.

25 26 27 28 29 — 987654321

Printed in the United States of America

Abraham never wavered in believing God's promise. In fact, his faith grew stronger, and in this he brought glory to God. He was fully convinced that God is able to do whatever He promises.
—Romans 4:20–21, NLT, emphasis added

However, before I experience the promise, I must walk through the process.

CONTENTS

FOREWORD

THERE ARE MOMENTS in life when faith is not just spoken but lived—tested in the fire of unimaginable trials and refined into something unshakable. This is the story of such a faith—a faith that endured the storm of stage four cancer while carrying the unbearable grief of losing a beloved son to the same disease at the same time she was fighting in faith for her life.

As her friend and pastor, I had the privilege of walking beside Michele DeCaul through every stage of this journey. I watched as she stepped boldly into her calling, saying yes to the Lord and being ordained as a staff pastor in our church. But soon after accepting this sacred assignment, life delivered a devastating blow, she was diagnosed with stage four cancer.

Many would have questioned, wavered, or even stepped back from their calling, but not her. Michele made up her mind that she would not take her yes back from God. Instead of retreating in fear, she chose to stand in unwavering faith, trusting that the God who called her would also sustain her. I witnessed the process of faith in action—through the pain of treatments, the heartbreak of losing her son, and the relentless decision to believe in God's goodness even in the darkest moments. And I rejoiced when Michele was declared cancer-free, a living testimony of God's healing power.

But her story does not end there. Out of her suffering, God birthed something even greater. It has been one of the most rewarding experiences to see her turn her pain into purpose—launching a foundation to help others battling cancer and establishing a Cancer Care ministry at our church that is now impacting the lives of patients, caregivers, and survivors. What the enemy meant for harm, God has used for good, and Michele's testimony continues to bring hope and healing to so many.

I Can't Take Back My Yes is not just Michele's story; it is an invitation to trust God through the fire, to believe when everything in you wants to give up, and to stand firm knowing that His plans are greater than our pain. Her journey is not just about surviving—it is about thriving, overcoming, and using her testimony to bring healing to others.

I pray that as you read these pages, your faith is strengthened, your hope renewed, and your spirit reminded that God is always faithful.

—Riva Tims Watkins
Founder and overseer, Majestic Life Church
Orlando, FL

FOREWORD

THERE'S SOMETHING IN this book for you.

I work as a collaborative writer, helping authors organize their ideas and their words into a book. When I started working with Michele, I didn't know anything about her. I didn't know whether she'd be sharing fluffy cliches or words that would anchor people during the storms of their lives. She calls herself an introvert, so why would she want to share with the world the details of the most challenging time of her life?

Michele and I spent many hours talking through her story. For months, we met in the early morning hours to process her life, write, and massage the words so that you, reader, could hear her heart and feel her message. She was vulnerable and raw, thoughtful and trusting. She shared details about caring for her son with cancer and then discovering that she herself had breast cancer.

I told her that I was superstitious and maybe a little hypochondriac, and all this cancer talk was making me worry about my upcoming mammogram.

We laughed about it.

Then we thanked God together when the results came back normal. That was April.

But then came May, and my sister, whose absence from my life would be inconceivable, who embodies the term sister in every sense, who lives next door, shared her own Stage 4 pancreatic cancer diagnosis. Suddenly, I was violently transported into a new world—a world no one wants to know first-hand. A world where one waits with bated breath for answers from scans, blood tests, and a medical team. A world where you're forced to look at death in the face to figure out how to live. A cancer diagnosis changes the whole family, not just the person plagued with it.

That day when this news felt like a boulder on my chest, I picked up my phone and texted Michele. Yes, my client.

It was a departure from the coach-client relationship we'd established. But I knew she would understand how I was feeling in that moment better than anyone else.

In our work together, Michele had given me permission to ask her all the questions that a reader would want to know about this time in her life—questions you would never ask a person you just met. She answered thoughtfully and authentically. She bravely went back to pivotal moments in her life and immersed herself in the questions, the fear, and the sadness over again. Tears flowed.

But now it was me. The tables had turned, and she began to coach me and help me process my sister's diagnosis. She helped me find my breath.

I tell you this story because it is a testament to how God moves in ways we can't even imagine and how He puts people in places to care for your spirit before you even know it's broken. I'll never get over how God uses a trial that one person endured to bless someone else who is going through it. Who but God could connect us in this way, at this time?

As we continued working on her manuscript, Michele detailed her conversations with God and vulnerably shared how she walked through what she calls the "dark corridor" toward a God who remained faithful and present. I learned first-hand how she faced fear, embraced love and surrender, and was able to push through with grace.

What I took on as another gig, turned into an unforgettable divine assignment. God had something more for *me* in Michele's message than I could have ever expected.

I tell you this anecdote because I truly believe there's something for you here as well. Out of all the books in all the world, you're holding this one in your hands. There's something unexpected for you in these pages. I don't know what you're facing. I don't know what the future holds. I do know that the testimony of a humble woman of God, who opens up and serves out of love and out of her hard-fought faith is going to bless you. I no longer doubt why this introvert is willing to open up her life, her journals, and her story in order to serve others who are facing a life-altering diagnosis.

What I discovered in working with Michele is that she's the real deal. She's not just a pretty face spouting religious platitudes. Her faith is authentic. Her words are true. Her heart is sincere and open to God and others. I know that God chose Michele to share her journey of saying yes.

As you read her words, open yourself up to what

message, principle, or nugget God might have for you in these pages. Whether you are encouraging a loved one or trying to find your way through a dark corridor, you are not alone. Michele's story is here to help you navigate your own.

There's something in this book for you.

—Delina Pryce McPhaull

February 2025

ACKNOWLEDGMENTS

WRITING THIS BOOK has been an extraordinary journey filled with pain and joy, and I'm deeply grateful to everyone who helped bring it to life.

First and foremost, I want to thank God. I passed "through the valley of the shadow of death" holding tightly and securely to His promises. He encouraged me with His peace, love, and lessons.

My family: Bryan, Carrington, Kayla, Mom, Dad, and my sister Debbie. You all served me, and it forced me to receive. Thank you for patiently loving me on this road of uncertainty. Thank you for your love that gave me the strength to fight.

Thank you to my inner circle (and you all know who you are): when I put a gag order on my family and each of you, you all surrounded not only me but also my family with unwavering love, support, and encouragement. Weekly prayers built my faith and brought me hope. The ongoing support was invaluable at every step of the process. Your love and belief in me kept me grounded throughout the journey.

A special thank you to Pastor Riva and Varian who provided the four hundred dollars needed for my mammogram that revealed the cancer diagnosis. Your thoughtfulness started the journey. Your guidance, insight, and support helped encouraged me to write this book five months into the journey.

Thank you to our friends Trish, Marc, Maria, Ed, Maureen, Torrence, Leilani, Terry, Ty, and Tony for your love and thoughtfulness during the loss of our son Bryan, Jr. Thank you for being at the hospital as a support to Bryan, Sr., and when I couldn't be there. Your support in so many ways helped lightened the weight of our loss.

Thank you to Alexcia, Bryan Jr.'s wife and her family for their care, love, and support during the loss of our son. Thank you.

Finally, I want to express my deepest gratitude to Delina, my writing coach, for her guidance and support in helping me organize my thoughts and emotions while writing this book. Your insight, patience, and encouragement made all the difference in shaping my ideas into a cohesive and compelling structure. Your expertise enhanced my writing and gave me the confidence to bring this "emotionally hard season" to life. Thank you for your invaluable mentorship!

Thank you, Jevon, my publishing consultant with Embolden Media Group, for your support, direction, and expertise throughout this publishing journey. Thank you for your keen eye for detail, vision, professionalism, and commitment to helping this book reach its fullest potential.

And to my readers—thank you for taking the time to read and share in my story. It's an honor to share it with you.

WITH ALL MY GRATITUDE,
MICHELE

INTRODUCTION

The thief does not come except to steal, and to kill,
and to destroy. I have come that they may have
life, and that they may have it more abundantly.
—JOHN 10:10 (NKJV)

THE DAY STARTED out like most days when my son, Bryan Jr., had a doctor's appointment. He had woken early and dressed in his Nike shorts, T-shirt, and loosely tied black sneakers. Knowing where he'd find me first thing in the morning—on the white, shaggy carpet in my office, immersed in prayer and devotion—he tapped on the glass door and peeked in. I motioned that I would be wrapping it up shortly and for him to start breakfast.

For four months, I had been the primary caregiver for him, my thirty-one-year-old bonus son, who had stage 4 testicular cancer. I needed all the faith, peace, and strength I could gather to remain focused and encouraged, so I finished up my reading, closed my eyes, and silently prayed, "Go before us today, God, and make this winding road straight. Give us peace as we interpret and process the reports from the doctor. Guide and order our steps as we step into this new day. Protect our hearts and minds. Grant us hope. Give us the courage to be strong, in Jesus' name. Amen."

It had only been a few days since he had been home after a two-week stay in the hospital for intense chemotherapy. The doctor had given him the green light to be home for the holiday, and Bryan was adamant that nothing was going to stop this from happening—and I mean nothing.

He was eager to get this appointment out of the way so we could continue preparing for Thanksgiving, which was in two days. He had been looking forward to spending the holiday at home with family, seeing the celebration he'd thoughtfully dreamed up come to life. He'd orchestrated every detail and handed out instructions for everything—down to who would cook the lobster tails and who would set the table.

After breakfast, we took the quiet drive to the hospital for his appointment. We arrived at the hospital to find no parking spaces available, so I headed to the parking garage, where I had to wind several stories to the top before I could find a space. As Bryan got out of the car and walked toward the elevator, I noticed he walked slower than usual. I hoped the stench of urine that assaulted us as we entered the garage elevator wouldn't upset his stomach.

His appointment went as planned. When he returned to the waiting room, the nurse explained we could expect some mild side effects from the medication they had just administered, along with the effects of the chemotherapy he had received forty-eight hours prior. She gave me a blue sickness bag, just in case.

On the way back to the car, I again noticed him walking slow—even slower than before.

"Are you okay?" I asked. All I could think was that we still had to take the smelly elevator back up to the car.

"I'm not feeling too good, Mom," he said.

"We're getting close to the car, and then we can get settled," I said, attempting to reassure him.

When we settled in the car, he looked pale—paler than his usual "cancer look" from the chemotherapy—and weak. I watched his stamina deteriorate before my eyes. Then he began gagging.

"Do you need some water?" I asked, quickly driving the car under the covered section of the parking garage, hoping to cool the car more quickly. The air conditioning was on full blast, but it was no match for the heat in our car that had been baking in the Florida sun for more than an hour.

No answer.

"Bryan, are you okay?" I asked again, this time with a little panic in my voice. "Do you need some water?"

It felt like time stopped, and my heart started racing. I looked at him in the passenger seat and realized his head had slumped to the side and his eyes had rolled back into his head.

I screamed his name at the top of my lungs. No response. I tried again. At that moment, all I could see were the whites of his eyes.

My mind raced. Was this it? Is this how his life would end? Was this the moment? What would I tell his father and his biological mother? What would I tell his wife? How would I explain that he died in my care?

I refused to have death enter under my watch. I had to take action.

I looked around the parking garage for help and saw someone sitting in their car, eating. I ran toward their car, hysterically asking for help. When they didn't move fast enough, I rushed to the emergency pull box on one of the cement columns and pulled it. The noise it emitted was deafening, so I started praying Psalm 23 as loud as I could: "The Lord is my shepherd, I shall not want. He maketh me to lie in green pastures. He leads me beside still waters. He restores my soul…"

I started reminding God of His promises and declared that Bryan Jr. would live and not die. As I prayed, I ran to the passenger side of the car, opened the door, and began calling Bryan's name again.

I watched his eyes roll back into position. I continued praying out loud, and he slowly answered. "Mom," he said. "What happened?"

All I could say was, "Thank you, Lord." With tears streaming down my face, I repeated, "Thank You, Lord. Thank You, Lord."

Then Bryan Jr. responded, "I know you brought me back from the death. I could hear you praying."

FROM DEATH TO LIFE

I've walked the dark, cold, and lonely corridors of death and felt the walls closing in. While I was the primary caregiver for my son, I also faced my own cancer diagnosis. This reality left me breathless. I felt like there was no one to talk to or reach for. In the death corridors, the walls spoke loudly, telling stories of defeat, fear, and dread ripped from the headlines. The lies seemed so true. They overpowered me.

I am not prepared for this, I told myself.

Then there was another voice, this one more still and quiet than the loud, bullying voice of death that echoed in the corridor. It was gentle, quiet, commanding yet safe. It called me to walk through this corridor, seasoning its words with love and safety. In almost a whisper, I heard, "I love you with a steadfast love. Nothing can separate you from My love, not even death. You are worth more to Me alive than dead."

Those words brought me back to life.

Sickness—and more specifically, disease—is an assignment from the enemy to rob, kill, and destroy a person's life. It comes to rob us emotionally through doubt, uncertainty, and fear. It seeks to rob us financially, adding to the stress of receiving required care. It can rob and torment us mentally with thoughts of death. It can rob us spiritually through anger that separates us from our faith in God. It wants to rob us socially by allowing us to feel alone on the journey.

When a cancer diagnosis is delivered, it's hard not to receive it as a death sentence. In fact, it can kill before we even begin to fight.

I offer you my story to let you know I've been there, as both a caregiver and cancer patient. If you are in the midst of a life-altering diagnosis, I want you to know I can relate to the stress, trauma, isolation, financial strain, and dark and hopeless nights. I can also relate to the fear, uncertainty, and loneliness of going through a health crisis.

But God.

God is here to give life—joyful, peaceful, overflowing, abundant life. Life that will be lived abundantly on earth but also eternally with Him.

Look for the Honey Moments

During my journey battling cancer, a faithful prayer partner called me every week to pray with me and encourage me. During one of our scheduled prayer times, she shared from Judges 14:8, which says, "When he [Samson] returned later to take her, he turned aside to see the carcass of the lion; and behold, a swarm of bees and honey were in the body of the lion" (AMP).

In this passage, Samson was able to kill a lion because God wanted him to know what he could do in the strength of the Lord. When Samson knew his strength, he would not be afraid to look his greatest difficulties in the face. My prayer partner shared from this scripture that as I journeyed through my experience, though it would be hard, allow the sweet moments to be like honey under my tongue.

This spoke to me, reminding me that we never know when a lion (like cancer) will be on our path, seeking those it may devour. However, when you believe like Samson, who defeated the lion and was able to find honey in the carcass, you will be provided with strength, immunity, and satisfaction.

Through this passage, I came to see that my faith in God would defeat the lion—be it cancer, fear, or death—while I learned how to enjoy, find, and eat the honey. In the process, my strength would be renewed. In the process, I would be refreshed with divine revelation for my journey.

Honey naturally remains sweet in order to preserve and support immunity. So when faced with this cancer diagnosis, I looked for "sweet" moments. Those sweet moments took me beyond my fears and into understanding. They nourished my soul and gave me the strength and energy to fight, even in the smallest ways. They acted as a defense or immunity against fear, hopelessness, and despair while bringing joy, gratitude, peace, strength, wisdom, and laughter into my heart.

The goal was to be continually refreshed and enlightened on the journey through the "sweet" moments I would encounter. It was God's will that through the challenges and the hard moments, my eyes would remain bright, my heart hopeful, my spirit nourished, my soul refreshed, and my appearance brisk as I endured.

Throughout these pages, you will see this symbol that denotes the recognition of a honey moment God gifted me on this journey. Whenever you see one, let it remind you to pray for God to open your eyes to see the honey moments He is providing for you as well.

Yes, in this book you'll hear my story, but I want you to hear more loudly the story of God's faithfulness, grace, strength, peace, and presence. I want you to know I've been there, but I want you to know, most of all, that God was there.

In the same way God's words brought my son back and revived my spirit in the corridor, my prayer is that this retelling of what God did for me will overflow into hope for you in your situation. I believe the thoughts, stories, and prayers in this book will help guide you to new life. I can't promise your health challenge won't end in death, but I can reassure you that with God, you can live each day in exceeding joy, peace, and gratitude. You'll start to look for the honey.

THE HARD YES

Cancer, for me, was a wake-up call that had the power to change me for the better or worse. It caused me to assess my faith and relationship with God and test whether I had enough faith to lead me through "the shadow of death."

Cancer slowed me down to simplify, reorganize, and reprioritize my life. I found myself letting go of things that didn't serve me, and I was motivated in new ways to stop wasting precious time. With cancer, some things just didn't matter. It accelerated my mission to break bad habits.

Cancer opened my heart to receive help, gifts, and support from others. It taught me to count my blessings every day. It caused me to face and conquer my fears. It forced me to care for myself like never before, pushing me to put myself first before others.

Cancer had me searching for meaning, value, and purpose so I could become the very best version of me. The close encounter with death prompted me to love and forgive the people who'd hurt me and be thankful for every day I was alive.

Sometimes yes comes easily. "Pack your bags. Let's go to the Maldives." Yes! "I want to give you a raise!" Yes!

"Don't cook tonight. Let's go try a new restaurant." Yes!
"Go have a seat. I'll do the laundry." Yes!

And sometimes life is a little more complicated. I
never said yes to grief, cancer, or death, but saying yes to
trusting God allowed me to say yes to Him even when
my life seemed to be falling apart. I can look back and
confidently say that knowing now what I would face—
the pressures of leading, caregiving, a cancer diagnosis,
loss of a business, grief—I wouldn't take back my yes.

God gave me the opportunity to say yes to the process of growth. I could have given up, stayed in denial,
and disappeared into my own thoughts. But because I
was willing to engage, I gained more than I lost. There
was so much light and peace, not just after the skies
cleared but right in the middle of the storm.

This book contains the lessons from God's Word that
I learned in the process. Each chapter includes questions to help you think about and journal your own
journey. Take time to thoughtfully answer them. I end
each chapter offering a sincere prayer for you.

I invite you to take this journey with me, to see God's
goodness in a fresh and new way, and trust Him more
in your situation. I invite you to allow this book to minister to you as you navigate the dark corridors of the
life-altering diagnosis you face.

Will you join me?

My Closing Prayer for You

*Dear Father, as I invite the person reading
these words on this journey You led me through,*

I ask that You be with them as You were with me. Touch their minds to understand Your boundless power and love. Bring renewal and insight into every crevice of their mind. Touch their eyes so they see possibilities and new perspectives to conquer every ounce of fear and doubt. Touch their heart so they come alive and extract a more profound love, joy, gratitude, and peace. May they not hold their life so tight they don't let You in. Tune their ears to Your voice so they can bravely walk through the dark corridors they face.

I pray they will hold Your hand as You lead them through illness and grief, for You are the way, truth, and life. As they read the words on the upcoming pages, may they come alive in hope and be healed in their mind, body, soul, and spirit, in Jesus' name. Amen!

Chapter 1

UNBREAKABLE BOND

MY HUSBAND'S VOICE had a strange sound to it as he said, "Miche, I've gotta tell you something."

Just a few days before, I had delivered chicken noodle soup to Bryan Jr.'s house, as he'd complained of flu-like symptoms for days. When he opened the door, he looked swollen and puffy, and I could hear the congestion and stuffiness in his nose when he spoke. I suspected he probably also had a bad sinus infection.

Two days later, he went to the hospital to get checked out. An emergency chest scan revealed fluid built up in his lungs, which was what had made it difficult for him to breathe. They drained the fluid from his lungs—and now my husband was calling me, sounding serious.

With his voice quivering, he said, "Bryan has cancer."

I let out a cry. How could this be?

When I hung up the phone, I paced the floor in my bedroom and cried, knowing our family was about to plunge into a hard season. Then my cry turned into prayer.

As my emotions quieted, I could hear a still, quiet voice say, "It's not unto death." Then Psalm 23:4 highlighted itself: "Yea, though I walk through the valley of the shadow of death, I will fear no evil, for thou art with me…"

The Earlier Years

I'd raised Bryan Jr. as my own since he was a toddler. When I met Bryan Sr., they were Bryan 1 and Bryan 2. They were inseparable. The love Bryan Sr. expressed for his son drew me to him. It showed me the kind of man he was—responsible, loving, and a committed family man.

I was just finishing up my master's degree when Bryan and I married, and my career as a social worker was just taking off. Mothering my toddler bonus child was simultaneously fun, scary, challenging, and exhausting. There was no on-the-job training for this. I had to figure it out and get to know him as we went. I said yes to being his mom without a manual or knowing all it would entail.

We were a busy household, especially after our daughters, Carrington and Kayla, were born. I became a stay-at-home mom and helped Bryan Sr. build his construction business.

We raised Bryan Jr. to be a person of faith, family, honesty, gratitude, commitment, hard work, and resilience and to believe in himself. Whether in school or in the jobs he held, he always did well and received awards. When he announced as a junior in high school, "Mom, Dad, I want to be an anesthesiologist," we knew he could do it. He was brilliant when it came to his studies. Nothing was difficult for him.

Whatever he set his mind to, I knew he could do it, and his dream became my dream. I locked in. I only realized later that I didn't give him the freedom to change his mind and take a different path—and then, after his first year in college, he quit school. The dream of a career in medicine had disappeared, and there didn't seem to be a new dream to replace it. At age twenty, he moved out and worked odd jobs. His focus shifted to making ends meet, rather than his future.

As a parent, I felt defeated. I didn't like that he had given up on his dreams, and the well of my disappointment was deep. I felt he was living below who he was created to be. In some areas, I felt like he settled. We'd given him every head start in life. Why was he dropping the baton and sitting on the sidelines? We'd raised him to strive for more, hadn't we? Were his choices a reflection of my parenting? Where had we gone wrong?

When Bryan Jr. moved out, I decided to live and let live. Whatever his choices from here on out, they would be out of sight and out of mind. As a young adult, he was creating his life, and I needed to keep my opinions about his life to myself. Outwardly, I was still his mom, supporting him however I could. If he needed feedback or direction on his career or finances, we would be there.

But those seeds of disappointment were still there, and it created emotional distance between the two of us. I didn't reach out as much. Thankfully, he and his dad maintained a strong bond.

A NEW ASSIGNMENT

In hindsight, I regret the years I unintentionally kept my son at arm's length. I didn't realize this until the reality check came from the oncologist; Bryan Jr. would need five rounds of intense chemotherapy to treat his aggressive stage 4 testicular cancer.

When we heard the treatment plan for the first time, we realized he would need care at home between chemotherapy treatments. At the time, I had a coaching business, which gave me a flexible schedule. I wanted to do what I could to help my son manage his care and beat the disease. I knew my yes was needed.

Even though I was saying yes to being Bryan Jr.'s caregiver, I also knew I would have to say yes to dealing with some of the unexpressed disappointments in my heart toward my son. Being a mom is different than being a caregiver. While in my role as a mom, I could nurture and guide, but being a caregiver was another level of service. I would have to lead selflessly and be genuinely supportive and patient, surrendering my way of doing things and my plans for how things should go. I would need to reach out to Bryan Jr. where he was, draw him in, and shrink the emotional gap between us.

I knew I was being pulled into an assignment. God was repositioning me to see what I couldn't see.

The first thing God showed me was how to clean up my heart. I wanted to rid my heart of my disappointments so I could serve my son wholeheartedly. Stewing over past disappointments would interfere with my actions, responses, and thoughts. God wanted His presence to shine through me to my son, and my unforgiveness was blocking the full blessing we could receive.

It's like this: Have you ever tasted a meal that wasn't prepared with love? A meal is a reflection of a chef's heart and passion for what they do, but if they have an off day, they can over-season or under-season the meal. When a meal is prepared with love, it is seasoned to perfection, leaving the person wanting more. *You can stir and prepare that food with anger or with love*, I heard the Lord say to me.

With an unclean heart, I could miss the details of Bryan Jr.'s care, miss what was important to him, or respond to him in ways that weren't seasoned with love. There was no escaping it. My heart needed to be softened, and I knew it.

A Clean Heart

In my study and prayer times every morning, I asked God for forgiveness and to transform my heart. I would read and meditate on Psalm 51:10: "Create in me a clean heart, O God; and renew a right spirit within me" (KJV).

As I went through this process, I discovered a few things. First, the process wasn't about my son but about me. I hadn't been ready to let him go as a young adult, and I hadn't make the necessary emotional adjustments as a parent. I thought his decisions were a reflection of my parenting. I was concerned how I would be seen by others and with having to answer the question "What's Bryan up to?" As a parent, I doubted if I had given him enough tools for success. Because he effortlessly succeeded in school, I thought he could have done more.

When God revealed the root of my disappointment had nothing to do with my son and was about me, I immediately asked for forgiveness in prayer. Through receiving God's forgiveness, my heart tenderized with love and truth, which brought healing. And when I removed all the expectations and judgments, it released freedom to love and gave me an opportunity to forgive myself.

I also got to see the work God had been doing in Bryan's heart. On our many car rides to doctor's appointments, we would engage in conversations. He would ask me questions about God. He would talk about his belief and how he had peace with whatever the outcome of this journey would be. He shared with me the books he was reading and how they built his faith. He shared his morning routine and some of his favorite scriptures.

I began to see him in a different light. I could see why God wanted me to forgive, and it was so I could see how my son was building his faith and learning more about the things of God through reading and meditating on scriptures. I witnessed a curiosity about spiritual things in him that I'd never seen before. He was asking questions and moving toward relationship with God.

God, through His grace, allowed me to see what I'd been missing when I had disengaged from my son and his decisions by relishing my disappointment. By keeping his life out of sight and out of mind, I hadn't been able to see how God was working in Bryan's life.

By laying down my expectations of what his life "should" look like, I was also able to see him for who he was, outside of striving for another goal. I had been hard on him, and when he resisted my "standards" and went his own way, I felt, in a way, like my presence in his life had no value. I thought he never got anything from me. But with this genuine and uninterrupted time we had together, battling through this disease, we shared unforgettable moments of pure joy—moments where I understood why God had chosen me to be his mom. What a gift.

I encouraged family members and Bryan Jr. to manage any unchecked negative emotions in their hearts too. If we were going to journey through this together, we needed to ask God to clean our hearts.

RELEASE UNFORGIVENESS

> "Father, forgive them; for they know not what they
> do."
> —LUKE 23:34, KJV

A cancer diagnosis is not the time to harbor unforgiveness. Unforgiveness, which resides in the heart, can contain bitterness, resentment, anger, loneliness, abandonment, rejection, pride, and a host of other emotions that are connected to a person or an experience. When unforgiveness is held in the heart, it is like being in prison. However, the prison is not for the person who may have committed the hurt. Instead, the person who holds the unforgiveness is the one bound.

Unforgiveness is the foundation for stress. Since unforgiveness is connected to our emotions, it can create unspoken stress in the body. When stress and cancer collide, this becomes a breeding ground for cancer to spread in the body. For example, during one of Bryan Jr.'s hospital stays, when he found out one of his colleagues had betrayed him, I counseled him to forgive his colleague so that anger, resentment, and bitterness wouldn't take root in his heart. "Nothing and no one else matters more than your well-being and health," I said.

We may not be able to control what others do to us, but we can control what we do to ourselves, especially in terms of how we allow their offenses to affect us. This is why God created an answer to unforgiveness. He knew the damage and impact it can have on our minds, bodies, and hearts. God's remedy for unforgiveness is forgiveness. Forgiveness is a mental, emotional, and spiritual action that protects our heart, soul, and body from being poisoned by bitterness, resentment, and offense.

Forgiveness is not a feeling but a powerful choice. It becomes a powerful choice when you courageously agree to forgive those who have hurt you. In some cases, people won't know or understand what they have done to hurt you. If you are waiting for them to apologize to you, you may be waiting for a long time. Therefore, forgiveness becomes the solution that expedites your freedom—freedom that releases you from your own emotional prison.

Do you recall when Jesus was on the cross, asking God to forgive His abusers (Luke 23:34)? He pleaded for the Father to forgive them because they were unaware of what they did to Him. He said this while He was suffering indescribable pain, nearing death, and innocent of any wrongdoing. He prayed for His enemies during the most difficult time, when He certainly didn't "feel like it." However, Jesus surrendered His feelings to obey God's principle regarding forgiveness.

> Bearing with one another, and forgiving each other, whoever has a complaint against anyone; just as the Lord forgave you, so must you do also.
> —COLOSSIANS 3:13, NASB

> "But I say to you, love your enemies and pray for those who persecute you."
> —MATTHEW 5:44, NASB

You see, forgiveness is an act of love, and Jesus showed us what love in action looks like by forgiving and praying for His enemies from the cross.

This principle challenged my heart. Was I ready to forgive those who had hurt me? For example, I could remember a time in my professional journey as a leader when my team would agree on a decision and direction for a project, but one person would work to sabotage and undermine the process. They pretended to agree but behind the scenes manipulated situations so their agenda and plans would be followed instead. It was so painful that I contemplated walking away from the position. But God wouldn't allow it. Rather, God impressed upon me to forgive that person and allow His grace to carry me through my weakness. My leadership was being tested, tempered, and tried by the fire of opposition.

Those memories stung. However, I knew now, more

than ever, I had no room to house bitterness or anger. I had to forgive.

But it wasn't a "one and done" thing. There were times during my cancer diagnosis when I had to forgive that person over and over again. My heart was so hardened toward them. As I laid my heart before God to forgive, He showed me my heart (ouch!) and eventually showed me their heart too and why they behaved the way they did. I began to feel compassion and understanding for that person. My heart softened.

Although the process of releasing unforgiveness was not easy, it was liberating not to have to carry that pressure in my heart. It was also liberating to know I would not be hindering my healing because of unforgiveness.

When I look at Jesus, who forgave the people who nailed Him to the cross, then I have no excuse not to forgive those who have hurt me. Besides, one offense is not going to be the only or last time someone hurts me, so practicing forgiveness is a benefit that works in my favor. I can, you can, and we must forgive everyone who has ever hurt us in order to experience personal freedom.

How Many Times?

So, how many times are we supposed to forgive?

In Matthew 18:21–22, we find Peter coming to Jesus with the same question: "Then Peter came and said to him, 'Lord, how often shall my brother sin against me and I still forgive him? Up to seven times?' Jesus said to him, 'I do not say to you, up to seven times, but up to seventy times seven.'" (NASB).

Does this mean we take the number literally—meaning 490 times? Did Jesus actually put a limit on the number of times we are to forgive? I can imagine someone with a notepad in hand, putting tally marks by the number of times they've forgiven a person, only to calculate and deduct how many times they have remaining to forgive. Well, I am sorry to say to that is not what Jesus meant when He said to forgive up to seventy times seven.

God never designed the principle to have a limit, and so the focus should never be on the number. Just imagine how many times we ourselves will need forgiveness. We have probably exceeded 490 times! Would we want a limit placed on us? This principle was created for us to forgive and keep forgiving.

Forgiveness doesn't give permission for people to treat you like a doormat. You can forgive people and still reserve the right to sever the relationship if it remains toxic or abusive. And when they leave your life, you must ensure they also leave your heart in the right way. Forgiveness is the key to this, providing healing and freedom for your heart and soul.

THE DAILY CLEANSE

My final note on forgiveness involves Psalm 51:10, which says, "Create in me a clean heart, O God; and renew a right spirit within me" (KJV). I had read this scripture probably thousands of times before—okay, that may be an exaggeration, but you get the point—and it read differently to me in this season of my life.

For the first time, the word *clean* jumped out at me.

David, the writer of this psalm, requested not a *new* heart but a *clean* heart—which means the one he had was dirty. Wow! This also means my heart is subject to being dirty. Every day, it requires cleaning.

When I think about having a clean heart, I think about the analogy of taking a shower or a bath every day. Most people don't leave their homes without taking a shower or bath so they smell fresh and clean. Just like bathing is important in our daily routine, so is having a clean heart.

Having a clean heart is done in prayer, through surrendering our hearts to God and asking forgiveness for anything we have done wrong in thought, word, or action toward ourselves or others. Then we ask forgiveness for that behavior.

Unforgiveness is a part of the dirt that can be hidden in the crevices of our hearts that must be cleaned out daily. When the heart is clean, we increase our ability to hear God's voice and receive His direction for our lives. A clean heart brings restoration and renewal and allows us to see our lives through a new perspective.

> Remember forgiveness is an act of the will, and the will can function regardless of the temperature of the heart.
>
> —Corrie Ten Boom

Your Turn

Forgiveness is not a feeling. It's a choice. Your feelings will change after you make the decision to forgive. When life is moving at a hundred miles per hour, we must slow down to check our hearts. This is not about being a good or bad person but a person who is aware of their emotions. When life is subject to change, knowing what's buried in your heart makes the journey easier. Who do you need to forgive today? Grab your journal and work your way through the answers to the following questions to get a sense of what God may be saying to you about this.

- Forgiveness is not just about others but also about forgiving yourself. What experiences do you need to forgive yourself for? Could it be the choices you've made, the lies you've believed about yourself, are placing unrealistic expectations on others?

- Take a moment and reflect on who you may need to forgive. Maybe they did not respect your boundaries, violated your trust, or betrayed you. Maybe they didn't believe in you and served as a discouraging and disparaging voice in your life. Who do you need to forgive so you can live more fully?

- Are you experiencing anger toward God for things that have happened to you? Do you find yourself angry at God for the loss of your loved one? For your health challenges? For your financial losses? Acknowledge your disappointments to God.

A CLOSING PRAYER

Father, thank You for Your daily dose of love, grace, and mercy. Thank You for giving us access to Your unconditional and unlimited love. It's in Your love that resentment, shame, guilt, disappointment, anger, and unforgiveness is removed and a clean slate is given. It's in Your love we find understanding, truth, strength, and healing. Through the process of forgiveness, sweep through, remove, and unblock our hearts from negative emotions. Thank You that there's nothing that can separate us from Your love. We thank you that it is through Your love and forgiveness that we can endure and experience freedom in Jesus' name. Amen!

Chapter 2

IN ALIGNMENT

THERE'S NOTHING LIKE being on the beach, taking in the smell of the salt air and the fragrance of sunscreen. I longed to hear the seagulls chirping, the waves rolling into shore, and the warm sun kissing my face. The beach is my place of retreat and renewal. Everything seems better at the beach, especially after the three years we'd just endured.

Bryan Jr.'s cancer diagnosis had been a gut punch. The tumor was located in the middle of his chest, above the lung and close to his heart, and the treatment for this rare cancer—one that only 3 percent of the population are diagnosed with—included many intense rounds of chemotherapy. Thankfully, the tumor had shrunk significantly, and we celebrated every victory.

This beach vacation on the Gulf Coast felt like an opportunity to truly exhale after hearing Bryan Jr. ring the loud bell a year earlier that announced his cancer was in remission. The sound of the bell was the sound of freedom. The sound of the bell was the sound of joy. The sound was sweet and his way of letting the world know the battle was over.

This vacation was an invitation for us to enjoy a

time of rest as a family. Bryan Jr. had made it a whole year without hospitalizations or chemo. He had moved back to his house, had started working again, and was engaged back in his life. It felt like it was finally safe to exhale. We allowed gratitude to well up and expand within us. We had a lot to be grateful for, and being at the beach was a great place to celebrate this win as a family.

An Unexpected Ask

After a long day at the beach, we returned to our hotel room for a quick shower before dinner. As I relaxed on the cool white comforter while waiting for my daughter to finish getting dressed in the bathroom, my cell phone rang. I saw Pastor Riva's picture pop up on my screen.

We chit-chatted a little, and then she made her ask.

"I was in prayer regarding the ministry and leadership ordination coming up in October," she said, "and God highlighted your name."

"Oh, really?" I began to feel uncomfortable about what she was about to say. While others might get excited about a promotion, I become hesitant because of what it will require of me.

"I want you to think about taking on the role of being a pastor," she announced. "You've already been doing the work, and you are well respected by the members. You are more than ready, and it's your next natural progression."

I listened to her in complete silence, thinking her words sounded like the same ones she spoke when I became an elder.

"Think about it," she said. "I know you are going to be great. Also, if you have suggestions on leaders who are ready to become ministers, please submit their names. I will check back with you soon."

I hung up the phone, shocked. I hadn't seen this coming. It wasn't on my vision board.

My husband, who was nearby when I got off the phone, asked if everything was okay, and I told him everything was fine. I wasn't ready to discuss it with him yet. I had to wrap my brain and heart around it, processing it for myself first, before sharing or deciding what to do.

I was honored to be asked, but I needed to count the cost, assess what would be required of me, and hear God's voice first. So, I waited.

EMBRACE ELEVATION

A praying mom raised me. Growing up, I watched my mom sit at the kitchen table with her Bible, her "Our Daily Bread" devotional book, her journal, and a pen. On Sundays, we went to church, and throughout the week, she listened to her favorite gospel programs with Dr. Robert Schuller, Billy Graham, and others. I credit my mom for her faithfulness and for intentionally creating a home where the presence of God was welcomed.

I went to a Catholic middle school outside of my district, and it was there I began to struggle with my identity. I was one of the few Black kids in an all-white middle school, so it was hard to feel accepted. Throughout public high school and college, I struggled with self-esteem, self-acceptance, feeling valued, and relationships. Even though I went to church and attended religious schools, I didn't have an intimate relationship with God.

It was not until I was twenty-seven years old, married, and already a bonus mom that I realized who God was and how, even without my doing anything, God had orchestrated blessings in my life and cared for me up to that point. His kindness drew me into a relationship with Him and inspired in me a hunger in me to want to know more.

By the time I was thirty-one and my oldest daughter was born, I was committed to that growing relationship and joined a church. God had given me understanding, confidence, faith, and wisdom from my earlier struggles with identity and belonging. I began to share from the overflow of the work God was doing in me.

As I became more involved in women's ministry, I discovered my purpose was to empower and inspire women to become the best version of who God called them to be. Through serving women, I developed a passion for prayer. As I grew in prayer, my faith grew, and my relationship with God grew.

I served in various ministry departments and in leadership positions without a title because of my love for serving others. Then, after some years, I was promoted to minister and served for five years. I was then promoted to an elder and served for two years. My passion for prayer was instrumental in developing an intercessory team ministry that helped govern and protect, the pastors, leaders, and church members through prayer. Hearing the results of transformation and healing, empowering women, and praying for others built my confidence, character, and commitment to my purpose. I felt God was giving me opportunities to serve that were aligned with my gifts.

This pastoral position seemed like the natural next step. However, I was afraid and hesitant to answer the call. I held it quietly and prayed for months. I knew this would have been a no-brainer for some, but I had to assess the requirements and responsibilities.

I asked God: *Is this from You? What is my purpose in this new role? Would the criteria and responsibilities allow me to fulfill my role as a mom, wife, caregiver, leader, and business owner? What impact would this have on those roles? How much time and energy would this take away from being with my family? How much time would it take away from serving my clients? Would I have the capacity to do what was required of me in excellence? Would the expectations be so great that I would fail others? How could I be a pastor and life coach? Would that be a conflict of interest?*

I wanted to honor God and the purpose He had chosen for my life, but I didn't want to burn out. I didn't want to serve others at the expense of neglecting my family or losing myself. Yes, this role would be a wonderful way to serve God and others, but was the timing in alignment with where God wanted me to spend my time and energy right now? It was a good idea, but was it a God idea? Was it for me at this time in my life?

I knew I couldn't make this move for any other reason than it was in alignment with God's plans for me.

About a month later, I received a voice message on

Facebook from Pastor Natasha, whom I'd only known casually. The message she left for me went deeper than any interaction we'd had up to that point:

> Minister Michele,
>
> I hope you are doing absolutely well. I just came out of noonday prayer, and I saw your face flash before me, and I heard the Lord say, "Embrace elevation." Don't second-guess the shifting, or don't reject the shift, not because you can't do it, because you are very strong-willed and very determined, and so whatever task is put before you, you will do it. But you have some reservations. I am not sure if it's because of people or because there will not be enough balance for the family. But the Lord said, "Do not reject the elevation, because I, the Lord, will smooth out the way." It is now time. It is the set time, and you must go forth. You must shift forth because there are people assigned to your shifting.
>
> If you don't shift, you leave people in the hallway. As you shift and submit to the shifted place, God will pull those with you that nobody else can take. God says, "Go forward." He has already made the way. "Move forward, for it is your new season. I am enlarging what you carry." As we are found faithful to a few, He makes us rulers. So there are many around that say they are available, but you are the one that is ready. So I pray the strength, peace, and joy of God. God will empower you to fulfill His assignment in this now season.

After hearing this audio recording, I was in shock. No one knew I was facing so many decisions. No one knew I had reservations about accepting the pastor position, especially because of the uncertainty of being able to spend time with my family. Pastor Natasha's words drew me into tears. Needless to say, this felt like God left heaven, came down to earth personally to answer my concerns, and then told me to say yes. At the very least, it took away all my excuses.

Still, I wasn't ready to give my pastor a confident yes or no. I needed more things to fall into alignment. I wanted to carefully and prayerfully go through my three-step rule that helps me organize and prioritize my mind, emotions, and life.

But first, I had to get through the planning of my "Emerging Women Weekend" event and continue to ask God for clear direction.

God's Amazing Power

In August 2021, I hosted the annual signature event for my coaching clients and other women looking for clarity and direction called "Emerging Women Weekend." Can you say *excited*? This was going to be our first time getting together since 2019, before the lockdown of the pandemic.

Now, is it just me or does it feel like anytime you're about to plan something great and give it your all, something always seems to slow you down, distract you, or throw you off? Well, that is what exactly happened. A few weeks before the event, Bryan Sr. got COVID-19, and I had to take all the necessary precautions so

I wouldn't contract it and miss my own event. Women were coming in from various states, and I couldn't afford to get sick or not show up. Could I do it via Zoom? Yes, but no! Could I bring in a few speakers? Yes, but no! Could I postpone it? No, no, no!

I dragged the twin mattress from the upstairs bedroom into my office and plopped it on the floor. That became my private quarters until it was time for my event. I had never prayed so hard for my husband's healing and my protection against the virus. From head to toe, I dressed in protective gear, serving his food and giving him vitamin C and orange juice from a distance so I would not be in contact with this contagious disease. With God's wisdom, I made it through unscathed.

After making it through that obstacle, I found out the night before the event that the venue had flooded and couldn't be occupied, and there were no other rental properties available. With only eight hours before the event was to begin, I informed the rental agent I was confident she would find me another property. I hung up and immediately went into prayer. Within twenty minutes, my assistant called to say the agent had located another property for us to use. I leaped with excitement, knowing God was behind the scenes working out every detail.

After all the obstacles, the weekend was a success. At the close of it, I was excited to see all the breakthroughs that had taken place among the attendees. As we ended our final session, I said, "There is one more thing I would like to share. You all know me as your life coach; however, over the last two years, I have been in the role of a caregiver, taking care of my son, who had stage 4 testicular cancer."

It wasn't my intent to share about the journey of the last two years, but because we ended on such a high, I wanted to add the cherry on top. The entire weekend, we had credited God for everything we experienced. It felt right to share what God had done within my family, winning the battle against cancer for Bryan Jr.

As I shared the story, their eyes opened wide. I could see their minds attempting to compute how I was able to do it. They had talked to me regularly and didn't have a clue what I'd been dealing with. In response to their shock and tears, I explained how God's grace and strength got us through the highs and lows of the journey and into victory. My story gave evidence and became a testament to God's amazing power!

THE SHOULDER TAP

I returned home on a high from that impactful weekend. But the next day, I got a text from a friend saying she had a dream I was about to step into a storm. She described the storm as a sandstorm. However, she said in the storm, there would be spoils or loot. When I read the text, I couldn't grasp the full meaning, but I decided to file it away until I prayed to gather additional meaning.

A few days later, I had an unexpected encounter I remember clear as day. I was walking down the hallway in our home to the garage, and I felt God tap me on the shoulder. I knew what the tap meant. God was calling me closer for a time of deeper intimacy and prayer.

I was resistant to obey right then because I felt the

time was inconvenient. I had recently experienced success with the women's weekend event, success and results with my private coaching clients, growth with the intercessory ministry, and success with various prayer classes. I wanted to continue to ride the wave of success.

But deep within, I knew I needed to be obedient. And so as I continued to make my way to the garage, I cried out to God with a loud, "Okay, okay!" like I was doing Him a favor.

About a week later, I began to get a glimpse of the sandstorm in my friend's dream. Bryan Jr. called to say he wasn't feeling well. He'd been having a dry cough and was going to schedule an appointment to see the doctor. In early September, his oncologist said the cough was due to fluid building up in his chest. The cancer had returned.

The news devastated us. I knew how much the first round of treatment had impacted him mentally, emotionally, and physically. But we were determined to win like we had before.

Processing the news, I asked myself, "Where do we go from here?" A still voice within me said, "Time to go into prayer." I knew God would use this as a catalyst to deepen my intimacy with Him. I may have dismissed the shoulder tap that had called me closer before, but God knew that as a mom, I wouldn't hesitate to enter the war room for my children.

A few days after we'd received the news, Bryan Sr. and I gathered the family for a discussion of decisions about Bryan Jr.'s health and financial concerns. We took the moment to encourage our son and his wife about the future, and we reminded them we would be there for each other as a family.

In that moment, I felt the nudge to share with everyone the invitation I had received a few months earlier to become a pastor. I also shared my concerns: How would it impact my role as a caregiver? What more would be required of me as a pastor?

Instead of being concerned, my family encouraged me to accept the promotion. I listened to their supportive words and remembered the voice message from Pastor Natasha who had assured me "God has smoothed out the way." I now felt the peace I needed to give my yes. Things were coming into alignment.

The next day, I called Pastor Riva and let her know I was ready to accept the call to be a pastor. She was thrilled. The ordination service was scheduled for October 17, 2021.

A LAVISH PROVISION

Before I officially started the new position, I focused on moving Bryan Jr. into our house again so we could help him as he received treatment. I also made a to-do list of the things I wanted to get done before starting my new responsibilities at the church. One of those things was getting my mammogram.

On the morning of my appointment, I made a video on social media singing, "It's mammo day!" to encourage other women to care for their bodies by scheduling their mammograms during breast cancer awareness month. My last mammogram had been in December 2018, and those results were unnerving because a small mass had been detected. We were grateful to find it was benign. Heading into my appointment this time, I was excited to be doing something proactive to take care of myself. After watching my son go through his cancer treatments, taking the proper preventative actions had taken on new meaning and a new urgency.

At the imaging center, I answered a few questions from the receptionist as she registered me.

"Your fee today will be four hundred dollars," she said.

Shocked, I repeated, "Four hundred dollars?"

When I had called to make the appointment, the scheduler informed me that for breast cancer awareness month, the fees were discounted to thirty-five dollars. I had been thankful for this discount because I didn't have health insurance.

The receptionist explained the special rate didn't apply to me. "I'm sorry," she said. "You will have to reschedule."

As I heard those words, they echoed strongly in my soul. I was ashamed and embarrassed to be turned away because I wasn't able to afford a four-hundred-dollar exam. I was being turned away for not being able to afford health care services? I had never been in this position before. I left the office feeling dumbfounded and defeated.

I sat in my car for at least an hour, trying to figure out how I could work harder to secure the money that was needed. It made me feel like I had to go harder and become more focused with my business so I wouldn't have to experience this moment again.

A couple days later, I shared my experience of the mammogram visit with my friend Varian and Pastor Riva. With lingering feelings of defeat, I shared that I needed to develop new business strategies to raise a steady flow of cash to ensure I would never be turned away again. They both listened and encouraged me. A few days later, I received a Cash App notification of money in my account for the amount I needed for my mammogram visit. I was overwhelmed with gratitude and immediately scheduled my next appointment.

Two weeks later, I was back at the doctor's office, recording another video that advocated for women's health and self-care and encouraging them never to neglect their exams. Then I entered the doctor's office, completed my registration, and paid my mammogram examination fee.

THE BIG DAY

Ordination day came, and I had mixed emotions. In the days leading up to it, I had been talking to God about the past two years. We'd endured the stress of a disruptive and exhausting pandemic. We'd contracted COVID-19. I'd experienced a month of unending headaches. My son was fighting cancer again. I was building a new business. The continual push without an end or any reward in sight did not feel good. I remember writing in my journal, "I love God, but these experiences I can do without."

Before getting dressed for the service, I sat quietly in prayer, relieving my heart of any anger, uncertainty, and unforgiveness to make room for God's wisdom. I could clearly hear God say, "My grace is sufficient for you, for my power is made perfect in weakness" (2 Cor. 12:9, ESV). When I heard this, I accepted the grace that was being given to me and settled in my spirit. I may not be in control of everything happening and I may not know the outcome, but since God's grace was being offered, I would take it, knowing His strength was brewing within me.

At the church, we found our row and filed in. Bryan Sr. sat next to me, and my daughter and her sister-friend sat adjacent to me. I watched as the deacons, ministers, and elders got ordained. My heart was overjoyed to celebrate with them. Pastor Natasha's message to me about embracing elevation replayed in my mind as the service went on. It brought my feelings and desires full circle; that even though I may not understand, I was where I was supposed to be.

When it was time for my name to be called, I stood up and my knees would not stop trembling. I was so nervous! As I stood on the stage, Pastor Riva called out my name and shared such heartfelt words about me. The congregation clapped and cheered, which was quite overwhelming. I was then asked to sit on the chair that was set on stage for those being ordained. Bryan was asked to join me.

Pastor Riva spoke powerful prayer declarations over me and laid her hands on me. She declared I would receive the impartation of all the great generals and leaders that had laid their hands on her during her years of ministry—the late Oral Roberts, Benny Hinn, the late prophetess Sheila Spencer, Apostle John Eckhardt, Apostle Joshua Giles, and others.

The most memorable and impactful moment of the service was when Bryan hugged me after the prayer of impartation. Even though I have had many hugs from him, this hug felt different. It represented, for me, greater levels of trust, love, support, and togetherness. When his arms wrapped around me, I felt I could let go, fully release, and trust him to carry me.

As I returned to my seat, my eyes still filled with tears, I got a glimpse of my daughter and her sister-friend also crying. My son, due to his health, couldn't be in attendance, but he watched online from home. My greatest place of peace was having my family's support and love in this decision. It was a picture of alignment.

How to Live in Alignment

My acceptance of God's call to be pastor of spiritual development at my church has allowed me to do what I am purposed to do, which is to develop and train individuals in building a strong identity, effective prayer life, and intimate relationship with God. I also get to teach them the principles of God's wisdom and how to develop responsibility in managing their thoughts, emotions, and behaviors.

Living your life in alignment means ensuring your actions, choices, and behaviors are consistent with your core values, beliefs, and personal goals. When a person chooses to live their life in alignment, they're prioritizing what is personally important. It contributes to and adds to your overall well-being by promoting balance in various aspects of life, including work, relationships, and personal growth.

The Bible speaks to having a life of alignment by emphasizing the importance of aligning one's thoughts, actions, and purpose with God's will and instructions. Mark 12:30–31 says, "'Love the Lord your God with all your heart and with all your soul and with all your mind and with all your strength. The second is this: 'Love your neighbor as yourself.' There is no commandment greater than these" (NIV). Above all, believers are called to align their entire being—heart, soul, and mind—with love for God, which is considered the greatest commandment. In essence, the Bible speaks to the importance of alignment in various aspects of life but always points back to a harmonious relationship with God and His purposes. This underscores that true alignment brings about spiritual growth, moral integrity, and a life that reflects divine love and wisdom.

When I received this revelation, I adapted this principle for every area of my life and found that it gave me inner peace, mentally and emotionally. Because I was authentically living a life that was true to my values and beliefs, I was free to pursue my purpose while feeling a clear sense of direction and intention. This alignment gave me the resilience to overcome challenges and replace doubt with focus and clarity. In my personal life, I attracted and maintained relationships with like-minded individuals who pray and prioritize God's direction in their lives. I've experienced an overall sense of well-being. I can literally feel it in my body when my life is in alignment.

When life is out of alignment, though, it's like driving a car that has its wheels out of alignment. The car endures uneven tire wear, steering problems, loose handling, car vibrations, reduced fuel efficiency, suspension issues, increased stress on the car, and major safety risks. Like a car, if our lives are out of alignment, it can create conflict and internal stress. This is one of the reasons I am committed to living my life based on Mark 12:30–31.

Through many experiences over the years, I have learned to make decisions by what I call the three-step rule, which I discovered through this passage in Mark 12. I live by this principle and regulate my life, decisions, business, relationships, and coaching by it. This three-step rule helps me organize and prioritize my mind, emotions, and life.

Step 1: Put God first.

Genesis 1:1 says, "In the beginning God (prepared, formed, fashioned, and) created the heavens and the earth" (AMPC). In the beginning, God. And in the beginning, unconditional love. God's unconditional love sets the foundation for me to find purpose and build my life. With God at the beginning of my life, I get to discover, create, build, and maintain it.

I establish and secure a relationship with God through prayer, devotion, and reading the Word of God. When I spend time with God, it ensures He is with me in my identity, parenting, marriage, health, business, ministry, and relationships. Outside of my time of devotion, God provides me with wisdom, direction, and things I need to make it through the day. The principles I learn through God's Word help me prioritize and organize my life, develop and maintain good character, and provide insight so I know how to effectively function and respond to life situations. Through His principles, my confidence grows so I can face difficult areas of my life.

When my life is faced with uncertainty, challenges, disappointments, tragedy, adversity, poor choices, accomplishments, rewards, and recognition, I look to God to determine my instructions and responses. When I look to God, He, rather than my emotions or the opinions of others, determines my decisions. I stay focused and value God's divine presence above all else and refuse to throw Him aside or use Him out of convenience. I find great comfort in funneling my life through His principles.

Step 2: Care for myself.

This second step opens me to understand and receive the unconditional love God has for me. God jealously loves not only me but also you. With the love He gives us, He wants us to discover, honor, respect, affirm, love, and value who we are in Christ.

I align my identity with who God says I am so I am not being redefined by my past experiences or failures or by the opinions and expectations of others. Daily, I make the conscious decision to take care of my mind, body, and spirit. I give myself permission to take care of myself before caring for others. I give myself permission to discover my purpose and what I am called to be and do in the earth so I can experience personal fulfillment and freedom. I commit to care for myself and appreciate everything about me so I am not dependent upon others to affirm or appreciate me. I see the good in me so I can see and honor the good in others. This is true self-care as guided by God, and when I am living in connection with who I am, I can love and serve others and live authentically.

Step 3: Love others.

As shared above, honoring and loving ourselves comes before we can love others. It's not always easy to love ourselves first, and that's because we fear not being loved, accepted, and approved by others. But when we can fill up on God's love and see ourselves as valuable, then we will have enough fuel in our love tank to love one another. With the love we obtain from God and for ourselves, we can encourage, inspire, empower, and correct others as needed.

Experiencing and receiving love for ourselves first helps build our confidence, esteem, and character as we interact in our relationships, which include parental, marital, business, friendship, and other people we may come in contact with. Fueling up on love makes it easier to offer compassion, understanding, support, and forgiveness and to extend grace to others in the face of disappointment, disagreement, adversity, loss, life changes, and other life interruptions. Healthy relationships provide support and belonging, which is needed for our success. Learning to love others reflects and shows our love relationship with God.

I encourage you to consider adopting this three-step

rule to help empower, organize, affirm, and give yourself maximum freedom.

Your Turn

How often do you set aside time for self-reflection to assess if your actions align with your core values and beliefs? Here are a few questions you can consider so you remain focused, resilient, authentic, and fulfilled.

- Who are your strategic and meaningful relationships that support and reflect your true self and your aspirations?

- Can you identify habits or behaviors in your life that may hinder your ability to live in alignment with God's purpose for you?

- Think about a major decision you're facing. How can you apply the three-step process to your decision?

- Do you feel at peace with the person you are today? If not, what aspects of your life would you like to change to grow your inner peace?

- How do you measure personal success? Does this measurement align with your innermost desires and happiness?

A CLOSING PRAYER

Father, we thank You for Your wisdom that teaches us how to align our lives through loving You, ourselves, and others. We surrender our thoughts, intellect, and emotions to align with Your principles. We thank You that alignment is an inside-out principle that brings our thoughts and behaviors in step with Your revelation and knowledge. We ask to experience freedom from doubt, confusion, expectations, and the opinions of others. We know that by loving You first, ourselves second, and our relationships third, we are fulfilled, strengthened, equipped, empowered, and victorious. When we operate according to Your principles, we experience clarity, instructions, direction, joy, peace, and endurance. We want to live our lives in order. We thank You for how You empower us to shift our lives into continual freedom, victory, and blessings, in Jesus' name. Amen!

Chapter 3

CHOSEN

As I made my way to the lobby of the medical center, I could feel Bryan Sr. watching me through the front windshield of his truck. The pandemic rules prevented him from coming with me to see my primary care physician to hear the results of the breast biopsy I'd had a week earlier. It had only been ten days since ordination day with all the applause, celebratory remarks, and overwhelming support from my church. I was riding that wave of celebration and was sure I would get reassuring news from my doctor.

I was wrong.

"You have breast cancer," the doctor told me.

Her words rang in my ears as I made my way toward our parked car. My thoughts were scattered. It didn't feel real. As I exited the building, my head was in a cloud and my heart pounded. I tried to hold it together, but as I stepped off the sidewalk, a wave of emotion crashed me to the ground. My knees buckled, and I doubled over on the hot black asphalt, tears streaming down my face.

Bryan saw me collapse and hurried over. "What happened, Miche? What happened?" He rubbed my back, and I could hear the urgency and concern in his voice. "What did the doctor say?"

Through sobs, I managed to mumble, "I have breast cancer."

Gently, he helped me up from the ground and over to the car.

I began to calm down and share with him what happened—that the doctor had opened my file, pulled out the report, and began reading all the numbers, measurements, and medical jargon, and then finally said, "Michele, you have breast cancer!"

I said, "Bryan, I heard her, but I didn't hear her. I stared at the skeletal picture on the wall as she talked, but all I could hear was 'Wah-wah-wah-wah,' like the adults on *Peanuts*."

I told him my focus wasn't on the diagnosis but on Bryan Jr. and the impact this news would have on our family. I also had no insurance. What impact would it have on us financially? The financial cost of this journey and the emotional and financial pressure it would put on my husband made me weep.

I thought, *God, why? Why have You chosen me for this battle? And why now?*

My thoughts raced, but I continued to tell Bryan about the appointment. "And then she prayed with me," I said. I told him her unsolicited request to pray for me was a sign God was with me.

In his strong yet sensitive way, Bryan said, "It's going to be okay. We are going to get through this."

In the past, when anyone in our family was faced with a tough situation, it wasn't unusual for my husband to cry. For example, when he found out Bryan Jr. had cancer, the weight of a father's love overcame him. I would console him, and his body would collapse on me like dead weight.

This time, God strengthened Bryan to hold me up. I knew it was a sign of God's presence when his countenance was extremely peaceful during this exchange in the parking lot. He was able to bear the weight of my news. God was with us.

My Job Season

Bryan and I had driven separately to the appointment because he had to return to work. As I drove down the road, more reality hit me. I called my friend Varian to tell her the news. Even though she was in the middle of work calls, she said, "I will meet you at your house. I am on my way."

When I got home, I greeted Bryan Jr., who was sitting at the kitchen counter. In a daze, I walked to my bedroom. With my back to the wall, I slid down to the floor, sobbing and asking, "How does this happen? Where did this come from?"

My mind still raced with thoughts, and the tears kept rolling down my face. Then my phone rang. I saw it was Pastor Riva, whom I knew Varian had called to tell the news. I answered, and her energy and joy poured through the phone. She reminded me of how strong I was and the things I had walked through.

"Woman of God who walks on water!" she said. "Woman of God who walks through walls and has been through the fire! You are going to make it through this! God will use this to increase your anointing!"

She gave me such an inspiring message, and it sounded good but landed flat in my spirit. I was numb. My emotions couldn't process all that was happening, much less receive her exhortation.

Though I wasn't able to process it at the time, I do remember two things she said that caught my attention. First, she said, "Didn't you ask for greater anointing to heal the sick and to prophesy with accuracy? Here is the path in which you will pass through." And second, she said, "This is going to be your Job season."

Job was a blameless man who feared and loved God, and walked in complete integrity, faith, and trust in Him. God chose Job because He knew Job's character and how much He could trust Job. God gave Satan permission to test Job but not to take his life. However, in the process, Job experienced his loved ones dying, the loss of his possessions, and a breakout of terrible boils on his body. Through it all, he trusted God and was rewarded with double in the end.

The words my pastor spoke strangely felt right, even as tears rolled down my face, because this meant it was more than just a diagnosis. It was about endurance. My mind swirled with emotions, and internal questions surfaced. I couldn't fully comprehend it all, but I understood what she was saying: I had been chosen!

I told Pastor Riva that I appreciated what she shared, but the truth was I had some questions for God. They were questions like: *Why? Why, after saying yes to being ordained, was this happening? Why couldn't I have maintained my old role and gone through this quietly without the promotion? Why did I have to receive this news four days after my twenty-seventh wedding anniversary? Why add more on me now and make me more visible with this new title? Why add more on my family as we have been supporting and watching Bryan Jr. endure his fight? Why add more emotional weight and pressure on us as a family? Why—when I don't even have insurance to obtain care?*

After I hung up with Pastor Riva, the doorbell rang. I opened the door and there was Varian, standing on the other side with open arms. I dove right into her arms and sobbed, hugging her in silence while my warm tears streamed down my face.

She showered me with hope and encouraging words. She shared with me the story of her mom who hid her breast cancer diagnosis from her and her siblings for years. In secret, her mom had taken a pill that treated the cancer and it has been in remission for years. This was another sign of hope God was sharing with me.

I shared with her that my fear wasn't about the diagnosis but the financial cost. I had watched my son's medical bills pile up, rising upwards of a million dollars, and I knew this had the potential to empty our savings account and cause us to lose our house. A cancer diagnosis doesn't just affect a person's physical health. It also causes major impact on a person's mental, spiritual, emotional, and financial health.

I didn't know where to begin to count the cost of this experience. All I knew was it was going to cost me something—just like Job! With no insurance and not being able to come up with four hundred dollars just weeks earlier, I was going to be in trouble.

Varian brainstormed ideas and researched ways to secure insurance, coming up with a strategy to pay for the appointments in the meantime. As she threw out ideas, I could feel a peace come over me. With these options available to me within hours of receiving the news, this was another way God was showing me He was with me. Though I had been chosen for this journey, I wasn't alone.

A CHANGE OF PERSPECTIVE

For two days, I sat in the pit, crying. sad, and I was sad and imagining the worst. But by the third day, I rose in a revelation that spoke to my heart.

God had chosen me. He was alerting me to give me the strategy to win. He was alerting me to get me ready for one of the biggest battles I would face. He was letting me know He was choosing me because He wanted to demonstrate His glory through me. He reassured me He knew that no matter what, I was going to trust Him. He let me know He was choosing me because of the unseen potential within me. His plan from the start was for me to win.

Once I settled on the notion of being chosen, my perspective began to change. One definition of *chosen* is "having been selected as the best or most appropriate." Another is "one who is the object of choice or of divine favor; an elect person." Now, biblically, the definition of *chosen* revealed itself when God made a choice among all the people He created and set them apart to execute the important purpose of His providence. When He chose them, it wasn't on account of their extraordinary merits but because God wanted to illustrate His glory to all mankind through them.

It's easier to accept being chosen when it looks exciting and favorable. But being chosen when the odds look uncertain or as if they are stacked against you requires a change of perspective. I remembered when I had walked down the hallway and felt the finger of God tap me on my shoulder, alerting me to seek Him. I had thought it was inconvenient at the time. Now I knew He was not only alerting me, but also preparing me for this very moment and for the months that would follow.

Adversity has a way of getting our attention and drawing us closer to God, doesn't it? Even though I felt distracted by the initial call to get away with God at the moment He tapped my shoulder, I am grateful He did. Now I knew something sweet awaited me on the other side of the dark moments.

I was chosen.

This revelation became my foundation. With God's power, I was able to shift my perspective. Not that it was easy or wouldn't require ongoing work, but for that day and in that moment, I decided it was time to win. If I had been chosen for this, it was time to fight and win!

When I shifted my perspective, I knew immediately my win would only take place from within as I fought my fears, doubts, and emotions. I knew I couldn't allow any psychological mumbo jumbo or religious babbling. I would have to dig deep to override fears of the unknown to walk in faith. If God saw fit to choose me for this battle, it was obvious He saw something I couldn't. There was nothing left to do but to fight and win, no matter what lay ahead.

God chose me before I could even say yes. I was just catching up to Him.

Your Turn

Being chosen can come with doubts, fears, inadequacies, uncertainties, and insecurities during times of adversity or promotion. It's important to approach these times with prayer, humility, and an open heart, seeking wisdom and discernment from God as you embark on your spiritual journey. Here are a few questions that can help you assess and prepare for the journey.

- What challenge (adversity or promotion) has God chosen you to face?

- Knowing that you've been chosen, what are some of the fears, doubts, and insecurities you have to face or confront?

- What are some of the signs that confirm you have been chosen?

A Closing Prayer

Father, we thank You for each day that is filled with Your grace and mercy. Today, we declare we are loved and chosen by You. The shock of a life-altering diagnosis reminds us that life is subject to change at any time. In times like these, guide us in Your grace, peace, and insight. Even though we don't get to choose the burdens we carry or the battles we will fight, we know that when we're with You, You've chosen us to win. Shift our hearts and minds to understand and believe we are chosen for both promotions and hardships. Remind us we are equipped in You and that as we believe and trust in You, we will endure. Increase our understanding to know that we will become an inspiration and hope for others to endure the fight and live. We are chosen to win! We declare today that we are living examples of hope for others and a witness to Your amazing grace. I pray in Jesus' name. Amen!

Chapter 4

BULLIED BY DEATH

THE FIRST BATTLE I would face after realizing God had chosen me for this fight was the battle in my mind. The diagnosis, my Google research, the folders of information, the possible treatment plans, the possibility of surgery, and my own experience of being on the journey with my son—all of it felt like an avalanche. I would be lying if I didn't say I was afraid. I was afraid of losing my hair. I was afraid of the effects of the medication on my body. I feared the doctors were wrong or not giving me information that would help me make the right decisions. I feared the cancer could spread while I waited for treatment. I feared not seeing my children's future milestones.

One morning during my time with God, I was in my office on the floor in my usual prayer position. I picked up my cell phone to look up a scripture. As I went to Google, my eye caught the title of an article about a pastor who had just died of brain cancer. I clicked on the article and began to read the story about how faithful this pastor had been in ministry and how she had served her community. Many famous pastors, actors, producers, and the like knew her, supported her, and shared their kind remarks regarding her life.

I immediately felt anxious and overwhelmed. My eyes focused on the words *pastor, cancer,* and *died.* It felt like I was reading a story that could have been about me! That made the panic in my body rise and the thoughts swirl faster.

To pull these thoughts down and get myself out of my head, I actively responded with truth. The truth was I didn't know the details of this pastor's diagnosis, treatment, or medical history. The truth was I didn't know her position with God, nor did I know if she made peace with her outcome. The truth was only a fraction of the story was told in the article. The truth was her story was not my story. As I kept claiming the truth, it distanced me from fear and I felt a space of relief.

This was the type of daily mental work I had to do to detach from fear and defeat it before I spiraled into a mental death sentence. This strategy is named in 2 Corinthians 10:5, where it says, "We demolish arguments and every pretension that sets itself up against the knowledge of God, and we take captive every thought to make it obedient to Christ" (NIV). I held every thought captive and examined it against the truth so I would not fear what I saw.

After mentally moving through that, the hits kept coming. A few hours later, I opened my Facebook page and saw a post on my feed about a man who died of cancer. *Not again!* I clicked on the post and learned it was a local comedian who had come to our church on several occasions years ago. I remembered his humor and his stature. He was a big, bald guy with a funny heart. Seeing him in the pictures, slim in weight and looking completely different from how I remembered him, put me in shock. I read more and learned he had battled bone cancer for a few years. He had traveled around the world to get the best treatment, but on that day, he had passed away. His wife shared family memories and acknowledged all the people he made laugh. When I read his funeral was going to be on my birthday, my stomach sank. It was another targeted jab from the enemy, designed to harass me.

Reading these stories, one after the other, was not a coincidence. I believe the enemy planted those seeds of suggestion to take me mentally down a rabbit hole into a dark place so I would lose my focus and unravel mentally and emotionally.

When I saw that fear was once again attempting to bully me by sending me more messages of death, I had to resist. With the faith and little bit of strength I had in that moment, I repeated to myself, "My birthday will be a celebration of life today, every day, and for many more birthdays to come." I knew in that moment I would have to spend more time confronting death.

A couple days later, it felt like the enemy partnered with the algorithm yet again to show me even more posts about other people dying from cancer. In one story, I learned of a female OB-GYN physician who left behind her husband and two young children. The stories continued, and it confirmed the work I would need to do to overcome this situation—mind, body, and spirit. It would have to start from within. I couldn't control the ways stories of death would come to me, but I could control how I processed and responded.

The Battle With Fear

It became exhausting doing constant battle with my mind, though. More stories surfaced and increased my mental distress. One night, I dreamed a dark presence hovered over me and I couldn't speak. It was hard to try to wake myself up from this nightmare.

Worry threatened to overtake me as thoughts of death consumed me. With all the images, thoughts, and stories of death spotlighted around me, I became overwhelmed. I was in a dark corridor, where the walls spoke loud lies ripped from the headlines I'd seen. I knew many people died in the corridor because they listened to the bullying voice of death. I knew I had to find a way to quiet my spirit to hear the still, quiet voice of God—to hear His love and not the lie. But how?

One day, Varian called to check on me, and I shared the private encounters I was having with death and how it had created psychological warfare in my mind. She reminded me of a time when my emotions had tried to slap me around. Like a true boxing coach, she said, "Michele, are you going to let your emotions punk you? Are you going to allow your emotions to just slap you around?"

As she said that, I could feel my back get straight. I was unwilling to allow my feelings to punk me. Before I knew it, I was saying aloud, "I am not a punk!"

"You have to confront death by making peace with it," she said. "Allow yourself to be okay with death. Now, this doesn't mean you agree to die. But making peace with death takes the fear and sting out of it. It means facing the possibility of death before you go into battle. When you develop this mindset, you don't allow fear to punk you."

I could feel my fight coming back. I shouted, "I will not let fear punk me!"

She told me about the book *The Art of War*, which speaks about the importance of knowing your enemy. The enemy, in this instance, was the thought of death. "If you don't disarm death," she said, "you will die before you physically die because of the fear that lingers in your thoughts."

I realized that on this journey, fear could undermine my healing and limit my ability to speak and see possibilities for my life. Fear is the ultimate bully, coming with the intent to rob, kill, steal, and destroy. John 10:10 says, "The thief's purpose is to steal and kill and destroy. My purpose is to give them a rich and satisfying life" (NLT).

Faith and trust in God's promises becomes a defense against this highjacking. Once faith is received in our thoughts, it begins to alter our mind, thoughts, and actions. Fear keeps watching, observing whether it can come in by the measure with which you respond in faith.

I came to realize that rather than believing fear, God was calling me to a deeper level of understanding of the love He has for me. As it says in 2 Timothy 1:7, "For God has not given us the spirit of fear, but of power, and of love and of a sound mind." The key to releasing love to destroy my fears, then, lay in my belief in how much God loves me.

With this foundation, He led me on a journey through His Word that further reinforced this strategy:

> "I have loved you with an everlasting love: therefore, with lovingkindness I have drawn you."
>
> —Jeremiah 31:3, NKJV

> Who shall separate us from the love of Christ? Shall tribulation, or distress, or persecution, or famine, or nakedness, or peril, or sword? ... Nor height, nor depth, nor any other creature, shall be able to separate us from the love of God, which is in Christ Jesus our Lord.
>
> —Romans 8:35, 39, KJV

> There is *no* fear in love; but perfect love drives out fear, because fear involves torment. But he who fears has not been made perfect in love.
>
> —1 John 4:18, emphasis added

> The steadfast love of the Lord never ceases;
>   his mercies never come to an end;
> they are new every morning;
>   great is your faithfulness.
>
> —Lamentations 3:22–23, esv

> God's loyal love couldn't have run out,
>   his merciful love couldn't have dried up.
> They're created new every morning.
>   How great your faithfulness!
> I'm sticking with God (I say it over and over).
>   He's all I've got left.

—Lamentations 3:22–23, The Message

Christ may dwell in your hearts through faith; that you, being rooted and grounded in love, may be able to comprehend with all the saints what is the width and length and depth and height—to know the love of Christ which passes knowledge; that you may be filled with all the fullness of God.
—Ephesians 3:17–19, NKJV

After reviewing these scriptures on God's love, I began to wonder if instead of a fear problem, I had a love problem! Love was what I needed in greater measure if I was to defeat fear. The revelation of God's love that had served me in previous seasons wasn't enough for the battle I was about to face. Therefore, rather than living in the limitation of fear, I chose to refuel in my Father's love.

Refueling in Love

The revelation of God's love is what brings the confidence needed to defeat fear. The perfect love of God has the power to drive fear out of my situation and my life. Where fear had the assignment to limit me through the diagnosis of cancer, it actually became the invitation for me to draw closer to God. The closer I drew to God, the stronger and more powerful I became in the process.

Understanding the spirit of God's love lifted me beyond the limits of my own understanding and into a more expanded view. My belief about God's love allowed me to make my relationship with God more personal.

As a witness to God's love, I am an investment to God,

which means I am worth more to God alive and in good health so I can fulfill my purpose and share with others about His goodness. It's the love of God that favors me and sets me apart. God loves me so much that He made me a joint heir with access to the kingdom and all He has in the earth. Through God's love, I am entitled to kingdom benefits and all the blessings He has for me.

When I seek Him and His righteousness, He adds all things to me. The jealousy of God fights for me. I am that woman whom He is so mindful of, whom He made a little lower than angels and crowned with glory and honor (Ps. 8:5). My Father sees my worth, value, purpose, and future. My Father's love for me is extreme and abundant. I am His beloved daughter, in whom He is well pleased. I am on His mind, and He is always looking to see what He can do for me.

This is the confidence I have, and it ministers to me in some of my darkest hours. What I can't do in my own strength, His grace and mercy are enough to help me. I am never alone because His love is in my awareness. In gaining revelation about His love, I can never fail, for His love is unfailing.

Additionally, God's reputation over my life is at stake. It is in God's interest that I do well on this journey to live up to His name. God's love will move mountains on my behalf and cause favor to be upon me. Through His love, I become that bride whom God protects. Like a husband who loves his bride, God will comfort and protect me if anyone touches me. When I go back and remember how God has shown His love for me, I also see His credibility and track record. The love of God is like a vaccination that immunizes me from the lies and false prophecies of the adversary.

When I received this revelation of God's love as I processed the cancer diagnosis, it gave me a place to rest and not worry while He worked on my behalf. And as I grew to shift my perspective, I created a declaration based on John 15:4 that I recited every day, which said, "I am in Christ, and Christ is in me. I am cancer free, and I walk in victory!" Stating this aloud each day empowered me and increased my strength.

A Sound Mind

The last strategy needed to defeat fear was having a sound mind about the situation I faced. Having a sound mind is about having a disciplined and enlightened mind. Fear can blind the mind from seeing God's truth. It can stop the mind from receiving and producing, preventing it from seeing possibilities and flowing in gratitude. A sound mind is about my belief system and about having a superior understanding of God. When I don't have a superior understanding or knowledge of God, my stability, focus, and sustainability is impacted.

Without a belief system in God, I run the risk of failing on the journey before I start. If I don't allow my mind to be enlightened on how to defeat fear and death, I will not rise and experience good health. This will prevent me from passing through the shadow of death. Faith works by the revelation of His love and having a sound mind to receive it. However, having a sound mind requires self-discipline.

Self-discipline is the ability to control our feelings

to overcome our weaknesses. It is the ability to pursue what we think is right despite the temptations. Executing self-discipline over the weakness of fear requires constant meditation and practice until new information is believed and established in the mind. When the information is believed and established in the mind, the mind becomes enlightened, stable, and strong enough to refute any lies.

Below are more scriptures that helped me to refute the lies and build my mindset:

> Your thoughts are far beyond
>   my understanding,
> much more than I
>   could ever imagine.
> I try to count your thoughts,
> but they outnumber the grains
>   of sand on the beach.
> And when I awake,
>   I will find you nearby.
>
> —PSALM 139:17–18, CEV

> "For I know the thoughts that I think toward you, saith the Lord, thoughts of peace, and not of evil, to give you an expected end."
>
> —JEREMIAH 29:11, KJV

When I read these scriptures, the truths they reveal became a part of my belief system and gave me an unbendable focus and strength. I made them a settled reality that couldn't be uprooted or destroyed, no matter what I faced or endured. As I made them a settled reality, fear was driven out and love welcomed in so I could attend doctor's appointments, labs, scans, and treatment appointments accompanied by a strong belief and assurance of God's love.

I chose to believe so I could rid my heart of fear and replace it with the truths about God's love. This task was no one else's responsibility, but it was my responsibility to pursue a deeper understanding of love so I could rise as a warrior from within to defeat fear and death.

Here are some ways I was able to defeat fear:

- Renewing my mind by reading scriptures about having power, love, and a sound mind.

- Believing what I read and shifting my focus from fear to the power of God's love for me.

- Believing that nothing, not even cancer, could separate me from my Father's love.

- Receiving the revelation of how God was expanding my capacity and understanding about His love.

- Believing the promises of God's love for my life.

- Making God's words on love personal toward me by writing declarations and reciting them.

- Making God's words on love personal to me by visualizing the image of His love activated in my life.

- Experiencing God's love, which revealed my negative thinking, in order to bring victory over my fears.

- Viewing everything through the lens of love, which created a flow of gratitude in my heart and allowed me to rest in His promise.

Being bullied by fear can feel like living in a state of constant anxiety and apprehension. It's as if you're under the control of an invisible force that dictates your actions and limits your freedom. This emotional tyranny can lead to a sense of paralysis, preventing you from making decisions or taking steps forward. Physically, it might manifest in symptoms like a racing heart, sweating, or shaking. Mentally, it can cause self-doubt, helplessness, and isolation as you try to avoid anything that triggers your fear. Spiritually, it can entangle and pounce on your faith to make you believe you're alone and that God has abandoned you. Ultimately, being bullied by fear can significantly diminish your quality of life, leaving you feeling trapped and powerless.

When it comes to confronting and defeating the bully, you must say yes! Surrendering your life to fear, anxiety, apprehension, helplessness, or isolation should never be an option. Never partner with fear to diminish your quality of life and freedom. Instead, say yes to fighting for possibilities. Say yes to courage, faith, and resilience, and stand up against the bully.

Your Turn

Give yourself permission to embrace the strength within you to "punch" through the anxiety and reclaim control over your life. Every yes is a step toward victory against limitations and lies set by fear.

- Reflect on a time when you felt as though you were being bullied. Have you ever felt bullied by a diagnosis? What feelings did you experience when this occurred? What were some of the threats the enemy used to keep you in fear?

- What was the "bully" attempting to take from you?

- How did you break free from the bullying thoughts?

My Closing Prayer for You

Heavenly Father, I lift Your name up and honor You for Your unfailing love over the life of the person reading or hearing these words. They are Your child, and You created them in Your love. I declare that negative seasons and cycles of fears, torment, bullying, and death are conquered by the power of Your love. I declare that Your love conquers fear in their life. They will not focus on the shadow of fear and death but instead focus on the power of Your love, which leads to a realm of healing, deliverance, and victory. Your perfect love drives out all fear now. I declare they have love, power, and a sound mind. Their mind is enlightened with truth.

I declare that nothing shall separate them from Your love, for Your love moves mountains on their behalf. Pour out Your love, grace, strength, and insight so they can endure a cancer diagnosis or any other illness that threatens them. I destroy any lies, doubts, threats, and fears sent to hinder their fight or faith. I declare they receive abundant life in exchange for believing and receiving Your love. They will live and not die, and will be a witness and share Your goodness and glory with family and friends.

Though they walk through the valley of the shadow of death, they will fear no evil, for You are with them and will never leave them. I declare Your love rises in their heart and they become a warrior with Your Word. I declare Your steadfast love never stops flowing over and through their life. I declare the power of Your unfailing love draws them closer to You and Your righteous right hand leads them through.

Your love lifts them and brings them the confidence they need to overcome. I declare that through the lens of love, all things become possible because they believe. I pray in Jesus' powerful name. Amen.

Chapter 5

LIFE OVER DEATH

DEATH WAS LIKE a bully that came to torment me every day. I was like a defenseless child, anxious and afraid. Every day around the same time, the bully would come to threaten, taunt, and cripple me, backing me into a corner before taking my lunch.

I was a child, new to this cancer experience. As I showed up for the first time with this diagnosis, death sensed my vulnerabilities. It showed up to snatch my faith and courage, with the intent to leave me anxious, frightened, and scared. It would pick me up by my neck, leaving my feet dangling so I could feel no foundation underneath me.

Lonely and afraid, I knew I couldn't continue living like this. I know how important it is not to leave yourself open to fear mentally or emotionally. The enemy, who is the father of lies, will plant seeds of doubt, worry, confusion, loneliness, and death in the mind. Before we know it, we've created all kinds of negative stories that can bloom into a full Broadway play in our heads! When we make our negative stories the focus, we miss out on opportunities that allow our faith to bring hope.

Surrendering to the thought of dying, for me, meant walking it out by trusting God. Surrendering to God and not to fear allowed me to stop being controlled by fear. I had to surrender my fears and surrender my pain in order to trust God this way.

By not surrendering, I was putting myself in the position of being in control of my situation. But being in control was just an illusion. The reality was I had limited knowledge, expertise, resources, strength, and power to control my outcome. When I surrendered, I became aware that all knowledge, resources, strength, and power came from God. Being in fear only tied my hands and limited the power God was freely giving me.

CONFRONTING DEATH

To paint the picture of surrendering to the fear of death, I confronted my fear of death by asking myself a series of questions.

Q: What would happen if your life ended today?

A: I would be with the Lord in eternal life.

Q: What would you lose if your life ended today?

A: Nothing.

Q: What can death take from you?

A: Nothing.

Q: Do you feel like you served those around you well?

A: Yes. I served and loved as a daughter, wife, mother, and leader. Since I served well, death can't take that away from me, because my ability to love and serve has been marked in the hearts of those around me.

Q: What type of impact did you make with your life?

A: My life brought love, value, and freedom to others in the form of faith, prayer, hope, wisdom, strength, empowerment, and laughter. This can never be erased.

Q: Do you feel the impact you made in those lives will still be felt, even if you were to die?

A: Yes, because there have been times when others have said they can still hear the prayers, lessons, wisdom, and encouragement I shared and it still brings them encouragement and faith to take action. My legacy and what I brought to the world will live on past my death.

Q: Is God's love for you greater than the fear you are feeling?

A: Yes.

By the time I completed this mental process, I had just enough peace within me to marvel at and appreciate my responses. I had never taken the time to examine or take in the impact my life has had on others. When I sat back in that moment, I realized death couldn't rob, steal, or destroy what I had already imparted.

To be honest, it made me feel really good to know that. Whether now or years down the road, lives would continue to grow and become successful as result of an exchange they had with me. Whether I am in the earth or not, I know lives have been and will be impacted because I lived out my purpose, my love for God, and my love for people.

Following this epiphany, I could hear Holy Spirit say strongly to me, "Your life is more valuable alive than dead! When you live, others will live because of who I am within you!"

Hearing this was a game changer for me.

I realized this was how I would pass through the valley of the shadow of death and fear no evil and know God is with me. I surrendered and confronted death to get to the other side, and on that other side, I found truth and freedom. Confronting death forced me into that mental experience, and that's where I got the peace. I wasn't holding on to my life with clenched fists. I had peace for whatever the outcome.

One day, in my time of devotion and prayer, I received an additional revelation of God's perfect love, along with a worship song by Todd Dulaney that talked about death's inability to hold me down. This gave me a new perspective and strength. When I showed up the next day, I was ready for the bully to come. Before the bully could take my lunch, I gave it to him. And then I was free.

Enter God's Power

When you have a relationship with God, death doesn't always have a negative connotation. Although the process of facing death is uncomfortable, it gets us to a great life. Being in relationship with God makes the difference and elevates us beyond our limited ways of thinking.

Rather than depending on my emotions or my inexperienced thoughts, I learned to renew my mind by gaining a greater understanding of Scripture. I chose not to conform to what I saw on television, social media, or even some information given by my doctors. All that information is subject to change when God is involved. Defeating death required me to renew my mind daily and remind myself of the truth.

You see, the thought of death pushed me to the end of my strength and into the entry of God's power. I am too weak to fight what I can't see. I am too weak to fight what I never experienced. I am too weak to fight in my own strength. I couldn't, by will power, get out of the loop of my disordered thoughts. My mind constantly said, *This is not fair! Why did this have to happen to me? I don't have cancer in my family. I've never had as much as a hangnail or a cavity. I am faithful, and I serve faithfully. I pray and lead a prayer team. Why me?* But these thoughts made me weaker, proving I was too weak to do any of it in my own strength.

Defeating death began at the intersection of my surrender of weakness and my embrace of God's strength and power. Where I surrendered, God's power stepped in. I made room for God to orchestrate and execute His plans to bring resurrection life into my life.

God's enabling power is available to us so we can fight and receive strength in every situation. My surrender gave God permission to have His way in my life and in this challenge I faced. I agreed to allow God to simply be God. This allowed God to be God in any way He desired to be.

- I would let Him be the faithful God, whose love would renew me day by day.

- I would let Him be the everlasting God, who loves me so much He will not leave me but will always be there through the ups and downs.

- I would let Him be the sovereign God, wise enough to lead me, wise enough to direct me, and wise enough to know how best to answer my questions and my prayers.

- I would let Him be the mighty and awesome God, who would defend me from any uncertainties along the way.

- I would let Him be the healing God, who would heal me at any and every level— body, mind, and spirit.

The attack on my body became an invitation to a divine encounter with God that drew me in closer to Him. Defeating death became as simple as being in relationship with God. Prayer, spending time with God, believing, affirming, and reciting scriptures became my active tools for defeating death.

Make It Personal

When I read passages during this time like Psalm 91, I personalized them to affirm myself and give a response to death. For example:

> Michele dwells in the secret place of the Most
> High.
> Michele rests in the shadow of the Almighty.
> Michele will say of the Lord, "He is my refuge
> and my fortress;
> My God, in whom I trust."

> For He will deliver Michele from the snare of the
> fowler
> and from the deadly pestilence.
> He will cover Michele with His feathers.
> Under His wings, Michele will take refuge.
> His faithfulness is Michele's shield and rampart.
> Michele shall not be afraid or the terror by night,
> nor of the arrow that flies by day,
> nor of the pestilence that walks in darkness,
> nor of the destruction that lays waste at noon
> day.

> A thousand may fall at Michele's side,
> and ten thousand at her right hand.
> But it will not come near her.
> Michele will only look with her eyes,
> and see the recompense of the wicked.

> Because Michele has made the Lord her refuge
> and the Most High her dwelling place,
> no evil shall happen to Michele,

neither shall any plague come near Michele's
dwelling.
For He will give His angels charge over Michele,
to guard her in all her ways.
They will bear Michele up in their hands,
so that Michele won't dash her foot against a
stone.
Michele will tread on the lion and cobra.
The young lion and serpent, she will trample
underfoot.

"Because Michele has set her love on Me,
therefore I will deliver her.
I will set Michele on high, because she has
known My name.
Michele will call on Me, and I will answer her;
I will be with Michele in trouble.
I will deliver Michele and honor her.
I will satisfy Michele with long life
And show her My salvation."

This passage of scripture is loaded with promises that
affirmed my response against death. The world was
facing a pandemic, airborne COVID-19 and its variants,
monkeypox, RSV, and flu. I was aware of the importance of protecting my immune system. Now I had to
put those same principles in place to protect my spiritual immune system. I declared that plagues and pes-
tilence would not come near me or my family. I was
determined to prevent any attacks on my immune
system or to accelerate or invite death around me.

RECEIVE THE SUFFICIENCY OF GRACE

As I engaged this journey with newfound insight on how to defeat the death bully that taunted me, I was only able to stop the loud voices from the corridor with God's grace. After surrendering my fears, trusting God, and believing I would live, God's grace was there to help me to do what I was unable to do. In the most difficult times, it's easy to give up, especially when the challenge seems impossible and insurmountable. But then we remember 2 Corinthians 12:9, which states, "But He has said to me, 'My grace is sufficient for you [My loving-kindness and My mercy are more than enough—always available—regardless of the situation]; for [My] power is being perfected [and is completed and shows itself most effectively] in [your] weakness." Therefore, I will all the more gladly boast in my weaknesses, so that the power of Christ [may completely enfold me and] may dwell in me" (AMP).

According to this scripture, God's grace is sufficient to bring strength and power in weakness. When you're going through a life-and-death-altering situation, it's hard to understand how this is possible. It would make more sense to ask God to take the fear, pain, and disease away. However, God's grace challenges me to change how I pray. So, in addition to praying for healing, my prayers shifted to ask for His strength and power to go through this difficult journey.

I attempted to ask God to remove the pain and to heal me. However, this scripture revealed to me God doesn't always take away the burden or the pain. Rather, through grace, He will cause us to endure and will bring us to higher perfection of wisdom and character. Through this affliction, I was learning God's grace was sufficient to comfort, strengthen, and supply me with the power I needed.

I realized my focus had been on the outcome and treatment plan. Although God wanted me to be healed, His plan was laser focused on developing me in such a way that when I faced future challenges, I would be unstoppable in fulfilling His purpose.

So, what did I learn about grace?

The grace of God is the awareness and understanding of the limitless provision, power, and possibilities contained in God, but it can only be accessed through Christ. Grace is the enabling power of God that brings us into participating with God by faith to receive what we believe.

> May the grace of the Lord Jesus Christ, the love of God, and the fellowship of the Holy Spirit be with you all.
> —2 CORINTHIANS 13:14, NLT

> You then, my child, be strengthened by the grace that is in Christ Jesus.
> —2 TIMOTHY 2:1, ESV

Grace removes the pressure of worry and the weakness of doing things alone. Through God's grace, we are given His strength, power, provision, peace, and possibilities. When I trust and relax in God's strength, I follow and align with His instructions.

SURRENDER TO ENABLING GRACE

I can do all things through Christ who strengthens me.

—PHILIPPIANS 4:13

It seems impossible, when reading the above scripture, to believe anyone could do *all* things. In our own strength and intellect, we are limited. We find ourselves always coming up short on time, energy, resources, and/or relationships. If we made this bold statement to anyone, we can rest assured they would look at us like we were arrogant to make such an audacious statement. Not only that, but this bold statement can also ruffle the feathers of your enemies and cause them to stand in your way to prove you wrong.

Would you agree?

Some individuals will vet your experiences, your college education, your finances, and your connections to determine if you can truly back up your statement. They'll say, "You can do *all* things?" The truth is, in our human strength, it is impossible to do all things. However, when it comes to doing all things according to the things that are lawful and positive, as it relates to purpose and God's plan, we *can* do all things through Christ who gives us the strength.

What does all of this have to do with defeating cancer? God is all knowing, all powerful, and ever present. The things we are unable to do in our own strength, according to our purpose, His enabling grace empowers us to do. When we believe this, it takes away the fears and any limitations that appear in our lives.

Ephesians 6:10 says to "be strong in the Lord and in the power of His might." The Amplified Version says, "Be strong in the Lord [draw your strength from Him and be empowered through your union with Him] and in the power of His [boundless] might." The energy and strength I used to journey through this season didn't come from me. It came from God. The results in my life were because of the enabling grace that gave me the strength to make it through each of the five-hundred-plus days that followed my diagnosis.

- God's enabling grace allowed me to rise to the level required of this circumstance.

- God's enabling grace allowed me not to spiral into debilitating sadness or constantly feel defeated by fear or the thoughts of death.

- God's enabling grace gave me the strength to pray for my son while my body was racked with pain.

- God's enabling grace allowed me to believe for myself, despite seeing the decline of my son.

- God's enabling grace gave me the ability to go from a caregiver to a patient.

- God's enabling grace gave me the strength not to get stuck in my emotions.

- God's enabling grace gave me strength to balance my emotions and my faith.

- God's enabling grace gave me the strength to make some tough decisions concerning my health and my body.

- God's enabling grace gave me the fortitude to go through this season alone with Him.

- God's enabling grace allowed me to withstand the days when the levee on the damn of fear broke to attack my mind so I didn't drown.

- God's enabling grace allowed me to become vulnerable and to discover different parts of me as He stripped layers off of me.

- God's enabling grace gave me a new perspective and insight regarding death.

- God's enabling grace allowed me to read my Bible at a deeper level and to watch godly, Word-based messages that empowered me.

- God's enabling grace allowed me to align my thoughts with healing scriptures.

- God's enabling grace gave me strength to encourage and pray for others in my weakness.

- God's enabling grace gave me peace to go through all the testing, scans, and surgeries.

- God's enabling grace gave me the energy to make phone call after phone call, despite the denials, to secure health insurance and community resources.

- God's enabling grace gave me the joy and strength to laugh.

- God's enabling grace was with me throughout my journey.

There was no way I could defeat cancer on my own, in my own strength. But because God said I could do all things through Christ who gives me the strength, this was something I could do with His grace. As I walked through cancer with this scripture, it shifted my mindset to believe I *could* do this through God's grace. I was quite aware my thoughts, my experiences, and my emotions were limited. I needed the enabling grace of God for this journey.

SEE BEYOND THE DIAGNOSIS

Do you know how difficult it is to watch your child fight death while you fight for your own life? There was no way my mind could separate Bryan Jr.'s situation from mine without faith. When the weight of fear and death becomes heavy, only grace can provide strength. In my ability, I was too weak to do it alone, but God's grace gave me the strength to see what was possible for my life on the other side of this. I believed there would be life after this. I believed my purpose in life would become richer and even more fulfilling. I believed I would live to tell this story and that my journey would empower others.

God never focused on the cancer. His focus was more on His plan and my purpose in the earth. This journey was only going to make my purpose even more flavorful and impactful. Locked within purpose was God's plan to overcome the challenges and to overcome the world.

God's plans to work through me would have been left dormant if I had focused strictly on the cancer. Cancer is a light thing for God, and cancer is not bigger than my God. It was God's original plan to lead me through in His grace, strength, and power to remind me that He is with me. As I kept my eyes on what was above (heavenly) and not below (daily things in the earth), I learned to focus on God and not the cancer.

In John 5:30, Jesus said, "By myself I can do nothing" (NIV). This signified the unity Jesus had with God. He did nothing independent of God, but He did things according to the will of God the Father. Jesus knew He needed the grace, strength, and wisdom of God to accomplish His assignments. And if Jesus acknowledged He was unable to do anything without the instructions and authority of God, that confirmed even more that I, too, needed God's grace to see me through this journey.

The spirit of death comes to bring hopelessness, sadness, depression, loneliness, doubt, stress, weariness, frustration, and fear in an attempt to make a person a sitting duck. However, the grace of God paves the way for insight—insight that brings strength, and strength that brings power. Death is no match for grace because grace is backed and given by the all-powerful God.

Discover Your Covenant

A covenant is a promise between two people to perform a certain outcome. It's like a promise. God made a covenant with Noah after the flood that He would not destroy the world by flood again. God made a covenant with Abraham that He would make him into a great nation, bless him, and make his name great. God made a covenant with David that one of his descendants would be on the throne. No matter how unfaithful people may be, God is always faithful to His covenant promises.

There are three levels in which we can operate within the realm of the Spirit. The first, most ineffective way to operate in the realm of the Spirit is through our emotions. Our emotions vacillate and will not give us the direction or information we need to understand. It is the weakest platform because it is fickle. The second level, higher than emotion, is our reasoning. Here we are also limited to our natural thoughts and logic, which can fail us.

But the third and highest platform is through covenant. A covenant is not emotional and is beyond logic. A covenant between two parties is established and binding. Psalm 89:34 says, "My covenant will I not break, nor alter the thing that is gone out of my lips" (KJV). God does this because of His credibility and reputation. What I mean is God doesn't just protect His people. He also protects His name.

The more I read my Bible in this season, the more I became aware it contains promises, principles, and prophecies that bring revelation and empowerment.

When death was the hunter, I learned to read Scripture differently than I had in times past. I began reading it with deeper understanding, so it transformed me. It was about believing there are divine possibilities available to me through God's promises and principles. In my spirit, I knew that if God had made a covenant with Noah, Abraham, and David, He also made a covenant with me.

I locked in on what the Spirit had said to me: "You are more valuable to me alive than dead." When I understood and believed the faithfulness of God through the covenant He had with me, then my belief in the covenant promises could override the lies. I believed that even though this challenge had come to me, it was God's desire that I live. Because of my relationship with God, I would be made strong and do great things!

When I first heard those words, "You are more valuable to me alive than dead," they blew me away. What this said to me was God was not done with me yet. There was more impact that still needed to be made through my life and purpose. There were more people to empower, encourage, and heal through my life. Again, it brought me back to what God spoke to Noah, Abraham, and David. This was my covenant promise, and if I trusted and believed Him, I would see the manifestation of His promises unfold in my life.

Because of my covenant with God, I was convinced death had no power over me. I was convinced this was not my time. I would live, due to the integrity of God. This is covenant!

I wish I could tell you the promise happens overnight, but it doesn't. Hebrews 6:15 says, "And so, after

[Abraham] had patiently endured, he obtained the promise." Like Abraham had to patiently endure, Michele had to endure as well. The promise required me to go through a process. Within the process, patience and my continued participation (that's faith) was required.

When walking through cancer, any other illness, or adversity, it is important that you, too, find your meaning, value, and purpose. When you find these things, especially with God behind it, it keeps you fighting for something bigger than the adversity.

GOD DOES NOT LIE

> "God is not a man, that He should lie,
> nor a son of man, that He should repent.
> Has He said, and will He not do?
> Or has He spoken, and will He not make it
> good?"
> — NUMBERS 23:19

It's not only the words of the above scripture that are important but the person speaking them. That's what brings me confidence. God is faithful and true, and neither does He lie. I had the evidence of what He had previously done in my life. God's character had been consistent, trustworthy, accurate, and dependable. I had to remind myself of this so I wouldn't doubt it. Because I believed, nothing could stand in the way of His promises manifesting.

Let me touch on God's integrity just a bit here. God, as the scripture says, is not like man. He *became* man in the form of His Son, Jesus, but He is *not* man, meaning He doesn't have the character or the weaknesses of man. Therefore, He doesn't lie.

When God speaks, He must honor His promises because He is accountable to His word. God doesn't have a mentor or a coach to supervise what He does. He has His word that He must fulfill, and this word also holds Him accountable. When God speaks His promises to us and when we believe them and confess them, it's like God is speaking to Himself. When God hears His words being spoken back to Him, He protects His integrity by performing what He says.

God defends and preserves our lives. Our faith will cause God to defend His integrity and His credibility. God, within His power, can make what He says happen because He is a God of integrity.

> "So shall My word be that goes forth from My
> mouth;
> It shall not return to Me void,
> But it shall accomplish what I please,
> And it shall prosper in the thing for which I sent
> it."
>
> — Isaiah 55:11

It's important to remember God's word is trustworthy because God is trustworthy. For example, if someone were to tell me they were going to give me a million dollars, my first thought would not be on the money but on the person making the promise. I would vet that person's integrity before believing them.

You also have to believe in order to receive. If God

gives you a promise and you don't trust God, then you will not receive the promises He has for you. The problem is never with the promise. The problem is our ability to trust God. We build trust through encounters with God that help us know He is faithful and true, that He is a man of His word, and that when He speaks, that word accomplishes what it is sent to do. When God speaks, His promises are backed by His power.

There is no power that can defeat or override what God speaks. When God speaks, then He *does*! This is what I hold on to. I live according to what He has spoken, for it will be accomplished. Because of what I learned and believed, death lost its grip over me.

YOUR TURN

Have you ever felt bullied by death? Confronting it can empower you. By examining the impact and value you bring to the world and those around you, you can give the bully your lunch to take the sting out of death. Here are a few questions that can help you through that process.

- What would happen if your life ended today?

- In what ways have you served those around you (family, friends, community, etc.)? What contributions did you bring to the world?

- How have you found personal fulfillment from your purpose?

- How will you be remembered? Do you feel the impact you made in the lives of others will still be felt even if you were to die?

- Take some time to list all the ways God has demonstrated His love toward you. List everything, big and small, that comes to mind.

- After making your list, write a prayer of thanksgiving.

A CLOSING PRAYER

Father, we thank You that Your promises are backed by Your power. We declare that when Your words go forth out of our mouth, it doesn't return void. Your principles and promises are our hope and life. It is Your Word that builds security, confidence, and trust as we make our way to victory. We thank You for Your faithfulness that goes beyond what our eyes can see or what our heart may feel. We arise and declare that what You have spoken over our lives will come to past in Jesus' name, amen!

Chapter 6

PLANNING FOR PEACE

M Y FRIENDS KEPT asking, "What do you need, Michele?" I didn't know. My brain was scrambled with all the logistics needed to live my new normal. My spiritual armor was in place, and it was time to prepare a plan for battle. My surgery—I had opted for a double mastectomy—was scheduled for January, so I had a couple of months to get things in order to run smoothly while I recovered.

I took a few days to be in prayer, to focus on what I needed, and to create a plan—physically, mentally, emotionally, financially, and spiritually. If I was going to have peace and victory, I had to create a plan that I could see and follow. Having a plan prevented me from being emotionally distracted within myself and from being externally distracted by others.

THE INNER CIRCLE

I am a planner. I rarely move through life spontaneously. I am also one who tends to care for others more than I care for myself, especially when I'm leading. In this situation, I knew somewhere deep within me that if I was going to conquer and have victory over cancer, I would need to unplug from all my responsibilities and create a focused plan—and it had to start with the people that would support me as I healed. I called this select group of people my inner circle.

When it came to sharing the diagnosis with others, I knew I was only going to share it with a select group of people. I was fully convinced in this decision because when Bryan Jr. was diagnosed with cancer in August 2019, God gave the same plan. During that time, I heard strongly that this was not the time to share on social media but only to share with family and a few friends. God was clear this would be warfare and not a social gathering for onlookers who wanted coffee and a weekly update. This was my life, not a show!

I was also reminded that at the beginning of the year, Pastor Riva had shared with the members of the ministry that it would be a year where we would be slow to speak but quick to listen. In the experiences we faced, she said, whether adversity or persecution, we would need to remember to be slow to speak and quick to listen and not to allow our emotions to get the best of us. Honestly, in times of adversity, especially something like this kind of diagnosis, it's easy to flock to people for comfort, sympathy, support, help, direction, and pity, and to only go to God on the side.

Additionally, Jesus, who was accused and persecuted as an innocent man, didn't say a mumbling word to His accusers (Matt. 27:14). He didn't complain or defend His innocence. Likewise, I knew this was not the time for me to share or complain to others or be distracted by my emotions. Instead, again, I needed to be slow to speak, and I needed to spend my time locating the grace that would be sufficient for me in this bitter season. My instruction from God was to put the emotional weight of this season on God, not others. He showed me He was the only one who could carry me through it.

Still, I needed to surround myself with people. We don't get through things like this alone. I needed my inner circle to give me space to grow and understand the new person I would become as a result of this journey. I needed a team of people who would watch me grow in my weakness yet support me in faith.

Even though I had many well-meaning, loving people who cared about me, I was adamant that people not pity me or feel sorry for me. For me, pity has the potential to weaken my strength, causing me to settle and accept excuses. The goal was to remain in God and to remain focused. I didn't want my emotions to interrupt what God was doing within me. This meant I could not accommodate any feelings of unbelief in myself or from others.

As I prayed, God highlighted the team to me, and it included my immediate family, my parents, my sister, my pastors, my friend Varian, and two intercessors. I believe God gave a specific assignment to each person to support me on the journey.

Mark 5:39–41 confirms the need to have the right people in the room for God to work. It reads, "He went inside and asked, 'Why all this commotion and weeping? The child isn't dead; she's only asleep.' The crowd laughed at him. But he made them all leave, and he took the girl's father and mother and his three disciples into the room where the girl was lying. Holding her hand, he said to her, '*Talitha koum*,' which means 'Little girl, get up!'" (NLT).

When God gave me this plan, I knew in my heart it was going to be hard for other people, including my family, to understand why I wasn't going to tell the world what was happening with me. In their defense, I knew they were eventually going to feel the pressure of not sharing it with others, as people would begin seeing less and less of me. I asked them to honor my request and allow God to do the rest.

Even though there were probably other well-meaning friends I could have told about my diagnosis, I felt peace in the small group I had chosen. I didn't know why at the time, but I trusted God to lead me if I needed to make my circle wider. I didn't know what the journey would require of me, and I couldn't clearly see all the next steps. Therefore, I felt responsible to just follow Him daily and not lean on my own understanding.

WHY AN INNER CIRCLE?

In hindsight, I believe God wanted to surround me with a small team of people for the following reasons.

1. To protect my energy.

A small inner circle would protect my energy as it would require me to be nothing more than who I was. In the eyes of my inner circle, I wasn't a minister, pastor, coach, or mentor. I was simply Michele, journeying through this diagnosis and unknown season.

Sharing information with large groups generally requires more energy to manage and monitor expectations. Given the type of person I am, I knew I would extend myself beyond my limits and possibly feel obligated to respond and share updates if I shared with a larger group. The small group of people God instructed me to share it with knew me, required less energy from me, and wouldn't require more of me than I could give.

My inner circle was my support and my outlet. They kept my life moving when I couldn't. Varian helped me navigate conversations and interactions so I could manage my business and inquiries from others. My pastor called and reinforced what I was learning directly from God; time and time again, my conversations with her served as a reminder that this journey had spiritual implications as much as it was a physical health challenge. Her encouragement and spiritual guidance were more than mere words; they had substance.

2. To shield me from pity.

One of the things I knew from the beginning was that I didn't want anyone to feel sorry for me. Pity, for me, is a form of emotional weakness, and that goes against the nature of who I am. Even though I knew people wouldn't want to see me go through this, I didn't want their emotions to impact the strength I needed to get through it.

Another reason I had a disdain for pity was because if I allowed it to enter my space, I could fall prey to feeling sorry for myself. I could run the risk of being mad at God, serving up excuses, and letting myself off the hook from fighting. Self-pity, over time, can slip in and wear your emotional strength down without you even knowing it. I had to stay on guard and be alert.

Also, because I was a leader others may have depended upon for direction and support, I knew it would be hard for them to see me in a weakened state. In many people's eyes, a pastor and leader is supposed to be the strong one. By remaining hidden for a time, I didn't have to worry about managing their perceptions of how I was doing.

I am aware of the power of our emotions and what they can do when we give in and give ourselves over to whatever crisis we face. I made the decision to allow no pity as a form of protection so that I wouldn't undermine and mislead myself by emotionally making the wrong decisions. God didn't want pity to blind me from seeing what He was doing in my life. I realized this was just a snippet of something bigger God was doing, so I had to stay emotionally and spiritually focused. Even though I knew intellectually that I wasn't going to die, I also knew my emotions would ebb and flow and attempt to tell me otherwise.

John 12:24 says, "I tell you the truth, unless a kernel of wheat is planted in the soil and dies, it remains alone. But its death will produce many new kernels—a plentiful harvest of new lives" (NLT). Even though my situation looked like facing a physical death, I had to die, like the scripture says, to negative, fearful emotions so this could produce newness in my life. Eventually, this resolve would bring forth new life, new insight, and new wisdom that others could benefit from.

3. To allow me to grow.

I naturally, prefer to be hidden. I believe God created me this way. As an introvert, I refuel and grow in my private, quiet space. This space, for me during this time, would be in my bedroom.

Over time, it felt like God had placed me underground, hidden away from everyone and everything for a season. I was out of view of many people, growing in a dark, hidden place. Like the seed referenced in John 12:24, the growth of the seed is concealed for a time. It is concealed in the soil but is being watered and nourished by its owner.

Some plant lovers not only water their plants, but also talk to them to increase the rate of growth. Similarly, my devotion and the revelation of God's Word watered me as I listened to His voice. In my hidden space, I continued to grow stronger and stronger.

My strength was demonstrated by how I patiently held my story and process close until an appointed time. I journaled to capture details before I broke through the surface. My strength was being formed in my own weakness. In this dark, hidden space, I was shedding the outer layers of who I knew myself to be. I was dying to ambition, religion, old mindsets, fear, approval, acceptance, tradition, opinions, expectations, and so much more, in order to come into a deeper space and relationship with God.

During the time I was hidden, many didn't see me, but they heard me. I posted entries and recordings on social media randomly. I participated in meetings and client coaching over the phone. Because I was hidden, there were times people would say, "I need to hear your voice to make sure you're okay." Hearing my voice was like putting their finger on the pulse of my heart as I lay hidden in growth.

4. To fortify my faith.

Because I didn't share my journey with everyone, I was shielded from hearing the opinions of others, listening to others' ideas and remedies, and enduring empty, cold, or customary responses—things like, "God will work all this for your good," "If God did it for me, He'll do it for you," "If you only have enough faith, I am sure you will get well," and "God will never give you more than you can handle."

Whether these statements, in and of themselves, are true or not, often they can feel like religious platitudes. It is as if the person doesn't really understand what someone is going through and is just concerned with saying the right thing to check off a box.

With my inner circle, I didn't have to be concerned they would offer platitudes or canned responses. When they said, "I will pray for you," I knew they would. I knew I needed genuine, faithful, praying friends and family surrounding me.

God put my inner circle in position to guard, protect, and give me space to expand my vision to see my identity, faith, prayer life, boldness, confidence, and purpose grow and expand without the influence or distraction of others.

My inner circle fortified me with unbendable faith focus. They came with no expectation or pressure and supported my efforts to protect my mind at all costs. With the diagnosis of cancer, I knew my faith and my focus would be under attack. It was my responsibility to develop an unbendable faith, which began with guarding my mind and my words. All the schooling I received, all the prayers I prayed, all the prayer classes I taught, all the scriptures I read, and all the principles I believed in God's Word were now being tested. It was time for me to execute what I knew to be true about God by allowing the truth of His Word to rise in me and lead me through.

5. To lift my burdens.

When it came to my inner circle, they were my burden lifters. They were nonjudgmental and gave me the space to feel and acknowledge my emotions without chastising me about what my faith should look like. They offered me a listening ear and gave me the freedom to discuss my fears, but they did not allow me to linger or get lost in those feelings. Their loving, faith-filled responses provided fresh perspectives, encouragement, support, and hope. Their feedback at various times gave me strength and pointed me in the same direction, giving me peace. On days when doctors' reports and tests were inconclusive, they reminded me of other options and possibilities and how to choose peace. Even though no one knew what the outcome would be, my inner circle, through prayer and faith, remained unwavering, steadfast, and committed to making this burden as light as possible for me as I journeyed through it.

CHOOSE THE RIGHT PEOPLE

It's important to choose the right people to be in your inner circle. Imagine being surrounded by people who have the heart but not the capacity to lift your burdens. They end up becoming an emotional weight instead of lifting the weight of burden. They may become burdensome because of their lack of faith, because they're worrying about the outcome, or because they're complaining about the doctor's prognosis and treatment plan. They may be unable to endure the length of the journey. They may lose faith in God. They may stop praying when God isn't moving on their schedule. Being surrounded by individuals who want to be seen and not serve can become frustrating and interfere with a person's healing.

When I began my journey with cancer, my focus was on "I want to live!" But this journey, where I kept information within my inner circle, allowed everyone to see the work God did. I didn't want to diminish what God was doing by giving everyone the play-by-play. Keeping my health journey a secret allowed God to transform me like He transforms a caterpillar into a butterfly while in a dark cocoon. At the end, I would emerge as evidence of God's supernatural grace. No one else would be able to take credit for or tamper with what He did in my life or in my family's life. When it was time to emerge and share my story with the world, there would be no doubt about the miracles, signs, and wonders that followed me on this journey because I believed. I could say, just as the Israelites did, "Look, the LORD my God has shown me His glory and greatness, and I have heard his voice from the heart of the fire. Today I have seen that God can speak to me, and yet I live!" (Deut. 5:24, NLT, personalized).

WISDOM FOR RELATIONSHIPS

When cancer knocks at your door, it feels like a death sentence, leaving you with physical and emotional pain. Pain that is left unchecked or ignored can turn into bitterness, resentment, or anger. Cancer can bring so much pain that it awakens you to a new reality that you have not been exposed to before. It interrupts your life—but it can also be the reason you reawaken to living.

When a person is diagnosed with cancer, they can suffer in isolation and feel as though no one can hear or see them. Their emotional pain can restrict and suffocate them more than the diagnosis itself. This emotional pain can bring a person to the end of themselves. They might, due to pride or insecurity, try to be superhuman. Or they might find themselves in loneliness and depression, which can cause a person to lose their desire to live.

Human connection is important on this journey. It reinforces our need to belong and feel accepted. But our longing for belonginess and acceptance can cause us to consider others before ourselves when we are fighting for our lives. In this fight, we must realize we don't have the space to care for or manage the needs of others. Rather than fight to belong or feel accepted, we must fight to live. Therefore, having the right people on the journey with us is important.

I had my husband and my inner circle to support

me without any fear of rejection or of being misunderstood. However, I know not everyone will have the same support team, and we can't force people to be on the journey with us.

We must remember this cancer journey is different for everyone involved. For example, if your eating habits have to change because of your illness, that doesn't mean everyone else will change their eating habits. It doesn't mean you should become the spokesperson for healthy eating. Our fight will not be their fight. It's important we don't place unreasonable expectations upon the relationships around us. Unreasonable expectations can burden, strain, and create unspoken tension in relationships. Don't try to evangelize others. Rather, give people the space to be with their own emotions and feelings as they are with you. This is not the time to want everyone to experience what you're experiencing.

A Word on Boundaries

Boundaries are designed to protect your emotional immune system by keeping in the people and things that serve you well and keeping toxic things out. When your emotional immune system is under attack, it makes you susceptible to stress, distress, anger, and sleeplessness, not allowing you to make clear decisions about your health.

When you are going through a cancer diagnosis, be reminded you are at your most vulnerable. It's important you're not under the influence of someone else's control and expectations of you. We must be clear on the things we say yes to and what we say no to and not be pressured to do things out of a sense of obligation or wanting to feel accepted. If you allow a person of influence to pressure you to say yes to things you should say no to, it could land you in places where it's not healthy for you as you go through your cancer journey. It can make you too afraid to communicate your needs and feelings or even ask questions. It could have you accepting negative language concerning who you are and the outcome of treatment. It could have you feeling unheard, defeated, and working overtime, mentally creating stories that are not true.

Having the right relationships matters. Boundaries are fences, not walls, which means they can be shifted, adjusted, and moved at any time. Boundaries are negotiable and moveable with open and honest communication. It's not selfish to create boundaries around your values as you go through this. Instead, boundaries create a path that keeps you on the road to where you want to go: healing and strength.

How do you know you have the right relationships around you? Real relationships are those where you can be transparent and honest, flaws and all, and they don't leave or judge you negatively. Real relationships genuinely and authentically celebrate with you when you share good news, and they do so without jealousy, envy, or comparison. With these relationships, there is a consistent flow of honor over time and seasons. They don't have to agree with you, but if they love you, they will support you and your decisions without friction or tension.

There are four types of people when it comes to relationships in times of support:

1. **The overbearing one.** This is the person who is there to help you but dictates what you need and with very little consideration of your input. It's their way or no way!

2. **The follower.** This is the one who will follow your lead. They are there to listen and hear what your needs are. With a humble attitude, they follow your lead concerning what you need and how you desire to be supported.

3. **The emotionally disconnected one.** This person is physically present but emotionally in denial about what is happening to you. They find it hard to accept that you have been diagnosed with cancer. They are present but may not get all of your requests completed. They may forget at times because they are in their own head.

4. **The toxic one.** This is the person who makes you feel bad about yourself and the diagnosis. They may even think you had some cause for your diagnosis. They make you feel you're not good enough. They pressure you to become more or do more because they don't fully believe the impact of your diagnosis on your life. This relationship becomes exhausting and is not

sustainable because there's no room for communication, success, or growth. This relationship makes healing and recovery difficult because of the stress and tension that comes with it.

When it comes to relationships, especially when you're going through adversity, find and connect with people who get you. Once you find them, make them part of your inner circle, and cherish them for a lifetime.

THE PRACTICALITIES OF RELATIONSHIPS

Bryan and I were intentional about how we would prioritize our relationship during this trying time. We made an effort to keep our lines of communication open and to spend time together. Our son was in and out of the hospital, and Bryan Sr. still had work demands. We talked about his availability to go with me to doctor's appointments, but also how I was okay with other people sharing that load. We vowed we would not obligate or pressure each other to take on any tasks so we could journey through this unusual season with love and grace for each other. We talked about how we would honor my request to not share my journey with others. We held each other accountable with faith-filled prayers and words to keep us strong for the journey.

As a mom, I had to prepare mentally to relinquish my roles as caregiver, chef, housekeeper, and grocery shopper. When you have been in a role for some time because you love and care for your family, it is hard to give it up. Then I had to prepare myself to receive care.

My husband offered to take me to my doctor's appointments. My daughter Kayla said she would wash clothes, clean the house, and do some of the grocery shopping. My other daughter, Carrington, was away at college. She remained attentive and engaging through regular FaceTime calls to check on me. My daughter-in-love, Lexi, offered to get me meals of my choice, based on what I was feeling up for, and to run errands. In addition, she offered to arrange for her brothers and mom to assist with taking Bryan Jr. to his doctor's appointments. During Bryan Jr.'s hospital stays, my husband and Lexi alternated staying with him.

My sister became my house manager, organizing meals and giving everyone marching orders with tasks that came up. Twice a week, my parents brought over a dinner of brown stew chicken, rice and peas, codfish and plantains, and my mom's famous chicken soup. My mom offered to come over weekly to help with laundry. And Varian gave me the consistent emotional support of a friend and kept me laughing.

With everyone in place, my main responsibility was to rest and heal.

OTHER LIFE PLANS

They say "A man without a plan, plans to fail." I was created to win this battle, so I created a plan that spiritually empowered and inspired me!

> Trust in the LORD with all your heart;
>   do not depend on your own understanding.
> Seek his will in all you do,

and he will show you which path to take.
—Proverbs 3:5–6, nlt

The key words from this scripture for me were "Do not depend on your own understanding." Although I didn't know the path ahead, I decided to trust God and not my emotions. As I acknowledged and trusted Him, I began to see and understand the plan for my mindset, marriage, ministry, family, finances, business, faith, strategy, and supportive team.

The ministry plan

During the months of October, November, and December, before the January surgery, I continued my duties in ministry. I still attended service on Sundays, participated in weekly staff calls, led the prayer ministry and prayer calls, taught prayer classes, coordinated prayer events, and taught Bible study on Wednesday nights. I didn't want to abruptly stop performing my responsibilities but instead took time to close out projects and create team leads for the areas of my responsibilities.

While taking time at the beach in December, I asked God to highlight individuals who could assist with leading the prayer team during my absence in January. The Lord showed me two names, Minister Anthia and Minister Jennifer. Minister Anthia had been teaching Bible Institute for ten years, so I thought she could serve as the lead teacher for the prayer ministry. Minister Jennifer is an administrative expert and could serve to organize and ensure communication.

After the healing prayer call one evening, I called Minister Anthia and thanked her for serving and facilitating prayer. In that moment, I felt released to share the diagnosis with her. She was shocked and in tears to know I had to go through this. Even in her tears, she consoled and encouraged me. "You're going to win this battle," she said.

I went on to tell her I believed God was developing, strengthening, and expanding our prayer ministry team and that I was led to ask her to lead the prayer team during my recovery. After prayerful consideration, she followed up to accept the role. Not only that, but she told me she felt led to meet with me once per week for prayer. She'd journeyed through a similar battle and was a witness to God's glory and power. She had walked this road and she could understand my feelings and fears, validate my thoughts, and encourage me for what was ahead. She could hold my hand through it like only a survivor could. I welcomed her invitation to pray with me every Tuesday evening. I saw it as another sign of God's love and support on this journey.

The business plan

As an empowerment coach, I get to share strategies and tools that help women get unstuck in their identity. I help them gain clarity, confidence, and focus on their faith and purpose.

At the time of my diagnosis and at the beginning of my care, I had six active private clients with whom I conducted sessions over the phone. I decided to continue with these private clients and to schedule them around my doctor appointments, surgeries, and other matters. I also began thinking toward the annual "Emerging

Women Weekend" scheduled for July 2022. I wanted to make a plan that would be stress free, allowing me the space to care for myself while still being able to manage my business.

Creating a business plan kept me from becoming overwhelmed with emotions that would push me to give up my clients. In fact, maintaining my private clients gave me an avenue to express my purpose. It gave me joy and meaning to still perform in this role. Without them knowing my diagnosis, I was able to execute and provide the strategies they needed to succeed. In that season, my clients gave me life and reinforced my existence when everything else felt like it was falling around me.

The surgery plan

After meeting with my medical interdisciplinary team in November and December 2021, it was discussed that the tentative treatment plan would include surgery, chemo, and radiation. Confident yet nervous about treatment, I begin to wrap my mind around the tentative plan while leaving room for God to snatch me out of this nightmare with a miracle. I shared the information with my inner circle and completed all the online paperwork and pre-admission testing to prepare me for the surgery. With a date identified for surgery, I did research and reviewed paperwork on recovery procedures.

Next it was time to purchase post-surgery recovery items. On the weekend before my surgery, I went to Victoria's Secret to purchase compression bras for post-surgery recovery. I went there, but I didn't know what

I was doing or what I needed, and the salesperson was not much help. I left with one bra I wasn't completely satisfied with and two velvety-soft, comfortable jogging suits.

It wasn't until the gifts started arriving on my doorstep that I realized how unprepared I really was. The first surprise gift that arrived was from my sister. I opened the beautifully packaged box and found a canvas tote bag, mastectomy recovery robe, recovery bra, support belt, neck roll, back support cushion, post-surgical drain care kit, and cold packs. As I looked through the package, my eyes filled with tears because none of these items had even crossed my mind. It never dawned on me I would need these supplies. To know someone else thought about what I hadn't filled my heart with gratitude.

Days before surgery, an Amazon delivery guy knocked on the door to drop off a huge brown box and two smaller packages. The box was so big it took my son, husband, and daughter to bring it into the house. When we opened the box, we found the perfect gray recliner—my recovery recliner. Varian and Pastor Riva knew I couldn't lay flat on my back to sleep. I needed to be in an upright position for the fluids to drain properly. They researched and conspired behind the scenes to purchase my recovery recliner. In a separate package were several post-surgery items—snap-front medical shirts, black and gray spandex compression bras, neck rolls, and several pairs of skid-free socks. The other box contained a shower chair.

A couple days later, packages with surgical sponges,

surgical gauze pads, gauze rolls, hot/cold packs, safety pins of different sizes, a lounge back pillow, and edge pillows arrived.

For me, this felt like Christmas! Even though it was happening under adverse circumstances, it still felt like Christmas in my heart because others took time to thoughtfully give me things I needed—things I didn't even know I needed. I sat with tears streaming down my face and looked at all these items; my heart filled with joy that my friends and family would love me this much to think of me in the details. Those gifts were like God reflecting and shining His love upon me through my friends and loved ones, showing me that in the midst of all this, He was supplying my needs. Receiving these items gave me such a peace, knowing I would be okay, which to me was yet another sign of God's presence with me. The peace I had in that moment took away every ounce of worry.

The Bible says, "Three things will last forever—faith, hope, and love—and the greatest of these is love" (1 Cor. 13:13, NLT). With all the faith and hope I may have had in this experience, love made the greatest impact on me. When I saw God's love in the details, it strengthened my faith and gave me even greater hope. It reinforced His promises and allowed me to see how He was with me every step of the way.

The spiritual plan

I found myself on a journey that no one in a million years could have told me I'd be on. With no clear natural explanation, I positioned myself to seek and acknowledge God through prayer. Even with the number of years I'd spent sharing, praying, and ministering to others; carrying the title of pastor, with college degrees, awards, and certifications to go along with it; and as the primary caregiver to my son, I still knew nothing about how to navigate my own diagnosis. Even though I knew I would win, I positioned myself to acknowledge God for the specific path and plan to take. During it all, I was fully persuaded there was nothing and no one that could have directed me on this path other than the Creator of the universe.

Every time I felt myself standing at a crossroads, needing to make a decision, I acknowledged God. Every time I saw God in the great and small decisions, peace guarded my heart for the next step, result, visit, scan, and conversation. Every time I saw His presence operating in my life, I acknowledged and celebrated Him for His goodness. The more I acknowledged Him, the more I grew confident He would continue to direct my path. I knew that when I acknowledged Him, there would be a reward. I knew if I could stand before the gates of fear and uncertainty and acknowledge God in confidence, the gates would open for me.

Before I went to my first medical team meeting with the oncologist, breast surgeon, and radiation specialist, I depended on God to give me a plan for each area of my life. I thought of this passage in 2 Timothy:

> I call to remembrance the genuine faith that is in
> you, which dwelt first in your grandmother Lois
> and your mother Eunice, and I am persuaded is

in you also. Therefore I remind you to stir up the gift of God which is in you through the laying on of my hands. *For God has not given us a spirit of fear and timidity, but of power and of love and of a sound mind.*

—2 TIMOTHY 1:7, EMPHASIS ADDED

As I read this passage, the memories of what God had done in my life and where He had brought me began to stir my faith. I began to declare and affirm these things. In my journal, I wrote:

God is with me, and I have a sound mind regarding my health. In my weakness, God is making me strong. I am filled with joy because God is doing something great in me. The joy of the Lord is my strength. I am strong in my faith, and nothing will separate me from my faith or from God's love. I will not go through this circumstance in fear, but in love, power, and soundness of mind. God will give me the strength that I need. I will be ready. When things become too much, grace will be given to me. Through this, God will give me a new path, new life, new plans, and new strategies. This is not the end, for God has broken the power of death over me through His Son, Jesus Christ. God chose me, so I will not worry or be ashamed, for I trust and believe in the Creator. I will hold on to my faith, my teachings, and my lessons. Through the Holy Spirit, I will guard the precious truth that has been entrusted to me.

The Word of God cannot be changed, so I am willing to endure if it will bring salvation and glory to God. As 2 Timothy also says,

> If we die with him,
>   we will also live with him.
> If we endure hardship,
>   we will reign with him.
> If we deny him,
>   he will deny us.
> If we are unfaithful,
>   he remains faithful,
>   for he cannot deny who he is.
>   —2 Timothy 2:11–13, nlt

Faith is hard to hold on to when we face negative life challenges. But if we don't have faith, there is nothing to hold on to and nothing to hope for. Faith was what I had when it was hard to believe and when cancer seemed greater than me. When self-reflection, doubt, fear, insecurity, and thoughts of death collided, it was difficult to fight and overcome them without faith.

Faith is my confidence, assurance, and evidence of what is possible. My faith is all I have. When I find myself in my most vulnerable state, I turn to God for His strength, wisdom, and insight. Rather than trusting in others' opinions, doubts, or expectations, my faith becomes my peace and hope.

One thing I know for sure is that at the beginning of this journey, God tapped me on the shoulder to spend more time with Him. As He used this situation to draw me closer to Him, I did so in faith. Therefore, I chose to engage God on the journey by doing the following:

1. **Praying:** "Therefore I tell you, whatever you ask for in prayer, believe that you have received it, and it will be yours" (Mark 11:24, NIV).

2. **Reading His Word:** "If you remain in me and my words remain in you, ask whatever you wish, and it will be done for you" (John 15:7, NIV).

3. **Listening to His Voice:** "My sheep hear my voice, and I know them, and they follow me" (John 10:27, KJV).

4. **Resting in Him:** "Be still in the presence of the LORD, and wait patiently for him to act. Don't worry about evil people who prosper or fret about their wicked schemes. . . . For the wicked will be destroyed, but those who trust in the LORD will possess the land" (Ps. 37:7, 9, NLT).

Faith is what you have when all you've got is God, and so for me it was important to engage Him for this battle—especially because this battle wasn't mine; it belonged to Him. Therefore, a part of my spiritual plan was to engage God regularly along the journey in order to keep my faith strong.

Your Turn

Putting a strategy plan in place in times of adversity creates direction and peace. Having a plan of peace provides emotional, mental, physical, and spiritual help and can prepare you to get ahead of anticipated challenges. Having a plan can prevent feelings of overwhelm. It can help you break down areas of your life into manageable tasks, reduce stress, and give you something tangible to hold on to. When a plan of peace is put in place, it can strengthen your ability to bounce back, give you peace of mind, give you focus to be in the moment, supply you with rest, empower your spirit, and leave room to nurture your soul.

- Describe how you feel when faced with unexpected challenges or adversity, like a negative doctor's report.

- What are some of your strategies for managing stress so it doesn't significantly impact your daily life and well-being?

- Name at least five people who can be a part of your peace plan and a strong support to you. Describe why you chose each person.

- How do prayer and faith help you access peace in your life?

- Write out a plan to increase your peace, reduce your stress, and empower your spirit during this time.

A Closing Prayer

Father, Your Word declares in 3 John 2, "Beloved, I pray that you may prosper in all things and be in health, just as your soul prospers." We come in agreement with Your Word to declare that we will be in good health and our souls will prosper! It is for Your good pleasure that we prosper and be in good health. Surround us with loving, kind, patient, and faith-filled people who can uphold us. Surround us with people who can carry and lighten the weight of the burden and who can endure with us to freedom and victory. Grant us peace so we hear Your strategies after a diagnosis. Remove and clear the path to anything or anyone that will distract, obstruct, or hinder our peace. We declare that through Your peace, we can prepare and plan in advance to reduce stress and feelings of overwhelm. Show us a plan that will give us peace of mind, empower our spirit, cause our soul to prosper and be at rest, and give us a strong bounce back. We thank You, Lord, and ask all these things in Jesus' name. Amen!

Chapter 7

LOVE LIKE THIS

MY "GIRLS" WERE gone!

After working hard on building my self-esteem and self-worth over the years, my confidence in my identity was strong. I had grown to become unshakeable in my image, worth, knowledge, value, commitments, and choices. I loved how I felt in my clothes. I appreciated my body and its rolls, curves, lines, and twenty-plus years of baby fat. I enjoyed exercising to ensure I remained healthy. Bryan never complained about my body and neither did I.

As I have learned, "Life is subject to change!"

Now, after the double mastectomy, where I was once confident, I found myself thinking about my image. I found myself questioning my beauty and my body.

REALITY CHECK

Reality didn't kick in until I woke up from the anesthesia hours after surgery, felt the bandages wrapped around me, and realized what was there before no longer was. As the scripture says, people look at the outward appearance—and I did too! I looked down and saw nothing.

There was a big difference between making the decision to remove my breasts and seeing my body afterward. It felt and looked totally different. At the time of decision, I was focused on getting the cancer out of my body. My focus was not on my appearance, thoughts, emotions, or how it would affect me. Now that the surgery was complete, the reality that a part of me was missing overwhelmed me.

First, let me rewind. When I had the consultation with the reconstruction surgeon, she explained what was going to happen. After the cancer was removed from the breast, expanders would be inserted and sown to the chest wall. Every month, saline would be injected to expand the chest cavity.

She asked if I wanted one or both breasts removed. Before she could finish, I said, "Remove only the breast that had the cancer." Then she shared that if she removed one breast, she couldn't guarantee it would be symmetrical and aesthetically appealing. She also shared that removing both eliminated the risk of cancer cells remaining in the breast.

After thinking it over and talking it through with Bryan, the option to remove both breasts gave me the most peace. It was important to me that when I looked at my body, it would be aesthetically pleasing. I wanted no regrets. As a married couple, we had not been here before. Bryan was extremely supportive and left it to me to make the final decision of whatever felt good for me.

Going from decision to reality after surgery was a totally different experience. Looking down a couple hours after surgery and seeing the bandage lying flat against my body was a bit weird. Honestly, I was afraid to see myself without the bandages. A couple days after being released from the hospital, when Bryan had to change my bandages, I couldn't look at my breasts.

"In Sickness"

Bryan had to drain three tubes that hung from my sides twice a day. I felt so bad he had to do this. As tough as my husband is, he has a weak stomach when he sees blood. You can only imagine what it was like for him to drain these three tubes. We would laugh hysterically as he prepared to empty the blood and other fluids in the silicone suction bulbs.

He changed my bandages and took me to all my doctor appointments. When I thought it was too much for him—he was still working a full-time job, running multiple million-dollar construction projects with more than one hundred fifty workers—I tried to alleviate some of the pressure by going to my appointments alone. Then one day, the doctor's office called to confirm my appointment. When they didn't get me, they called him. That's when he realized I was going by myself. He said, "I want to be there with you at all of your appointments. Give me the dates, and I will work my schedule around your appointments." Going forward, I made it my duty to forward all of my appointments.

On days I was too weak to walk, he would walk me to the bathroom. Several of the medications I took had me running to the bathroom frequently—and when I say frequently, I mean frequently.

On one of those frequent visits to the bathroom, my

stomach hurt so bad from cramping. I had feelings of nausea and hot and cold flashes. My mouth began to water, and I knew I was about to throw up. From the room, Bryan asked if I was okay and if I needed anything. I told him I felt like I was going to throw up and needed the trash can. Because of his sensitive stomach, he came into the bathroom with a bandana over his nose. I started to vomit into the trash can, and in no time, he started to gag. The next day, we had such a big laugh, replaying how we maneuvered through that situation.

"In sickness" was a part of our vows, and I had cried like a baby when I said them. I tear up now too, thinking how we have kept our promises under the hardest of circumstances. When life is "better," there's no need for perseverance and sometimes no need to show love to one another or to God. But when life is "worse"—when you must persevere under trial and endure the test—it becomes an illustration of the love, life, and strength of a marriage. This is when marriages earn the victor's crown of life!

I will say this. I knew Bryan loved me, but this journey made me realize, like the Stephanie Mills song says, "I never knew love like this before."

THE "WORSE" TIMES

Above all, have fervent and unfailing love for one another.

—1 Peter 4:8, amp

> Love never gives up, never loses faith, it is always
> hopeful and endures through every circumstance.
> —1 CORINTHIANS 13:7–8, NLT

Our vows also say, "for better, for worse," and I can tell you this: The sacrifice, time, love, and commitment that is required during "worse" times is not easy. Yet it reveals the character, strength, and love of a spouse. It's in these times that the capacity of a spouse is tested and stretched. I am so grateful that after thirty years, my husband's love for me stretched to love me through my worst and weakest time.

"Worse" times can cause your home, marriage, and what you built over the years to crumble as though nothing ever existed. Thankfully, our foundation was tested and held strong through the storm of COVID-19, the pandemic, the cancer diagnosis of our son, my unexpected breast cancer diagnosis, and everything that disrupted our entire lives. This proved the strength of our faith and our relationship with God.

Getting married to the person we love doesn't guarantee or shield us from unexpected trials that test the marriage, but having a true relationship with God leads us into the "better." This trial of sickness, death, and grief didn't bring out the worst in us but instead brought us closer. When I felt fear, Bryan's faith responded and encouraged me. When I felt alone, he would crack jokes and make me smile. When moments of anger and sadness surfaced, we cried together. We found ways to laugh and appreciate all we have. Our gratitude allowed us to recognize and count our many blessings, despite the number of losses we faced.

Love is not just a word; it is an action that reveals our commitment. It's the trials of life that reveal our strength, love, and commitment to each other. Colossians 3:1–3 says, "Since then, you have been raised with Christ, set your hearts on things above, where Christ is, seated at the right hand of God. Set your minds on things above, not on earthly things. For you died, and your life is now hidden with Christ in God" (NIV).

LOOKING TO GOD

As a couple, this trial caused us to experience pain beyond what we could have imagined or prepared for. Nothing could've prepared us for this part of our lives. We were left not to look at each other but to look up to God to guide us through this. There was a time words of support didn't give us clarity or solid comfort or healing from the pain we felt. There were times we didn't have words for our pain, either, because the pain was different for both of us. In those times, the only response we could give each other was a gentle hug. After the hugs came the answers we could only receive from God.

Having pain without God is like having a lifetime wound that never heals. Just imagine having a deep wound that never heals. The yellow pus oozes, and when it attempts to dry up, you keep picking at the scab. When elements like water, heat, or cold touch it, it's a reminder the wound is still there. Even when you put on clothes, the touch of the fabric on the wound becomes another reminder of the pain. Pain without God leaves wounds open.

We didn't know if these trials came to test our

marriage or kill our marriage, but we were determined to pull together. We believed what doesn't kill us makes us stronger. Through our faith, this test matured us, changed our character, and increased our love for each other.

These are the truths I know in my heart. These are the words I can tell you in hindsight. But at the time, I have to be honest, my vulnerabilities as a woman started to surface. My thoughts started to get the best of me. I know men are visual beings, and my husband was seeing me like this for the first time. I couldn't imagine Bryan not loving me. His love, words, and actions for thirty years had consistently demonstrated love. But this situation gave me pause. Would this be too much for him? Would he ever see me the same way again? The wound sites were gross. And even after they healed, the reality was that my breasts were now gone!

In my mind, I thought surely Bryan was going to see me as less beautiful. I wondered: *Would he still find me attractive? Would he lose interest in me? Would he accept me like this? Could I accept myself like this?*

THE TEST OF LOVE

We never know how we will truly respond until the experience arises—and, well, here we were! When love is tested, love knows how to pass the test.

> Love is patient and kind; love does not envy or boast; it is not arrogant or rude. It does not insist on its own way; it is not irritable or resentful; it does not rejoice at wrongdoing, but rejoices with

the truth. Love bears all things, hopes all things, endures all things. Love never ends.

—1 Corinthians 13:4–8, esv

The love that comes from God knows how to transcend all situations. The love that comes from God doesn't focus on a person's physical appearance; God's love focuses on the heart. When a person's heart is yielded to God, love can bear all things and every circumstance.

Bryan's consistent nurture and attentiveness helped me not allow insecure thoughts to enter my mind. I could see how God was using this season of grief and affliction to draw us closer together in character, communication, and intimacy. When we had more than one reason to be frustrated, irritated, and angry, we became *more* patient, understanding, tolerant, forgiving, and grateful.

I remember a conversation Bryan had with my parents one day, where he said, "I wish she didn't say 'thank you' so much. She says thank you after everything I do for her!" It was funny to hear him say it, but I am so grateful for the sacrifices my husband, children, parents, and friends made for me. There were days I sat thinking of how appreciative I was, and tears would well up in my eyes.

Bryan was consistently loving toward me. Before work, he would serve me a light breakfast, complete the draining routine, and give me my meds. He would call me throughout the day and then on the way home to ask if I needed anything. Once he got home, he would serve me dinner, give me my meds, and drain my tubes again. I would get my kisses daily. He did this for months, and it was a such witness to me that he truly loved my heart more than my appearance. His love continued to witness to me in my sickness. I know without a doubt that Bryan's love aided in my healing process.

What I welcomed was that out of a "worse" situation, we were able to create something better. Prior to this season, I cooked at least four days a week. After being diagnosed, I relinquished my chef duties to Bryan and my adult girls. However, there were times eating was a big challenge, due to the medication I was taking. Every day, Bryan would come home from work and ask, "What do you feel like eating?" He would offer a selection of different foods or make his favorite gourmet ramen noodles and serve it to me in the recovery recliner. He made those ramen noodles like it was a part of a five-course meal! Whether it was Saturday soup, Sunday breakfast, afternoon drives, Netflix movies, or watching the Tour de France, tennis, basketball, football, or boxing, we found ways to stay connected and make the best out of a hard season.

As 1 Corinthians 13:7 says about love, "It always protects, always trusts, always hopes, always perseveres" (NIV). I was grateful to know that in our case, this applied to major life changes.

Loving Myself

But the question remained: Would I be able to love myself and once again have confidence in my appearance?

It took me three weeks to finally face the mirror once I could take my first post-surgery shower. I felt awkward and uncomfortable because I didn't know what to feel or expect. I stood in front of the mirror and peeled one eye open and then the next. To my surprise, it wasn't as bad as I had imagined in my head. I turned from side to side and then made eye contact with myself and affirmed to the new Michele in the mirror: "I'm going to be okay!"

For eight weeks, the recovery process was painful. I experienced muscle spasms, a burning sensation (my skin was on fire, especially at night), shoulder stiffness, fatigue, and nerve pain. I slept in a recliner for eight weeks to alleviate the pain and get the best rest.

For better or for worse, in sickness and in health, Bryan and I found ways to pull together. I am grateful I gave my yes. Not only did I have a loving spouse for the journey, but I also had the rewards of accepting and loving the new me.

YOUR TURN

Marriage is an intricate dance of prioritization, selfless-ness, and harmony, and love is the music that makes the dance possible. The love reflected in a marriage becomes the force that binds two people together, allowing them to face life's complexities as a united front. The love within a marriage is not just about romantic gestures, dates, or passion, but about selflessness, endurance, for-giveness, and growth. Selflessness is caring about the needs of your spouse more than yourself; it's being self-sacrificing. When it comes to endurance, love gives a marriage the strength to go beyond hardships and hard seasons. We don't look at the hardship but rather draw our strength from love. The spirit of forgiveness allows those in a marriage not to keep a score on the conflicts but instead to provide a clean slate to see every situation from a different perspective. Finally, love encourages personal and mutual growth as we adapt to each other's changes over time.

When love is at the forefront of a marriage, it acts as a powerful adhesive when challenges arise, keeping the relationship intact with strength, resilience, unity, and hope. I believe love builds resilience against external pressures that might otherwise lead to a breakdown. I believe love unites a husband and wife to ensure they work together to find a common solution rather than drift apart. Love provides hope, healing, and the belief that any obstacle can be conquered when those in a marriage stand in agreement.

In essence, love in a marriage is more than a feeling— it's the very essence that keeps the union strong, flexible, and everlasting.

- How have your struggles and challenges shown you a different side of love?

- In what ways has your illness changed your image of yourself? What insecurities have surfaced in the midst of your health challenges?

- In times of adversity, how difficult is it for you to receive and accept help from others?

- What are some of the ways your spouse has brought joy to your challenging journey?

- How has your spouse demonstrated their commitment to you through life challenges and changes?

A Closing Prayer

Father, we thank You for Your love, which makes us beautiful and resilient from within. When cancer comes to disrupt our lives, Your love comes to bring us hope. We are grateful nothing can separate us from Your love. When sickness, doubt, and worry arise, we can trust Your love will never fail but will strengthen us to endure. I pray Your perfect love will drive out fear and build resilience, confidence, and strength. I declare that marriages are connected and built upon the foundation of Your love that is self-sacrificing, enduring, forgiving, and growing. I declare that love within a marriage is strong, resilient, flexible, unified, and filled with hope. Let love be at the forefront of every individual marriage to withstand any external pressures so they can draw closer together to experience greater love, peace, joy, and freedom, in Jesus' name. Amen!

Chapter 8

BEARING THE UNBEARABLE

I WASN'T READY TO let my son go, and neither was I ready to hear the prognosis of his deteriorating health. My faith was strong in that I believed in my heart that my son and I would come out on the other side of this journey and would stand on platforms together speaking and encouraging others. My faith was so strong that I had a shirt made for him that said, "Miracle in the making." These words were screen printed in black lettering on an olive-green shirt. I believed he would be our miracle, so I had my husband take the T-shirt to the hospital to lay across his body. I knew without a doubt that God moves in response to faith and our prayers. My faith wasn't shaken, because I knew what God had done when I cried out to Him in that parking garage. God had brought my son back to life that day. I believed deep within me that if God did it then, surely He would do it again. I wasn't ready to move off my prayer position.

Even though my body, just weeks after surgery, was racked with pain, I continued to fervently pray for Bryan

Jr. It was all I knew to do. I prayed from my recovery recliner, and I prayed as though my life depended on it.

I prayed God would intervene and heal his body.

I prayed the doctors would return with a new prognosis and outcome.

I prayed my son would prove the doctors wrong and a miracle would take place in his room.

I prayed the cancer would dry up and no longer spread through his brain.

I prayed he would wake up and be responsive to the tests.

I prayed God would pour out His Spirit upon his body so new life could invade his weak body.

I prayed, "God, You sent Your Son Jesus for this purpose—to heal his body."

I prayed until I was physically weak.

I prayed so hard, with my heart heavy, that my tone changed, I began to sweat, and tears rolled down my face. My words were more pronounced, and scriptures that contained healing and life rolled off my tongue.

I texted Minister Anthia, an intercessor, for additional backup to support me in prayer.

I continued to pray—until I received the call.

THE LAST CALL

While sitting in my recovery recliner, I got the call from my tear-filled husband. It was after midnight, but the doctor had informed him our son had maybe an hour or so to live. The cancer had spread rapidly to his brain.

Shaken and through stammering words, Bryan suggested I gather the girls to talk to him one final time.

This was going to be it. Death was coming. In that moment, from my recovery recliner, with heavy tears streaming down my face, I texted my inner circle to pray for Bryan Jr. and our family.

I gathered his sisters, and we said our final goodbyes.

It was about to end, and I could do nothing, no matter how much I prayed, declared, and warred in my prayers. I did all I knew to do, but this time it wasn't working. My son was being taken away from me, and I wasn't prepared. As I sat in my gray recliner, watching from my phone on FaceTime, our son departed from the earth. All I could do was release a loud scream.

My mom, dad, sister, and Varian showed up at our house within the hour. No one had the right words to say, so they just sat with me and allowed me to cry. A couple weeks earlier, my husband, daughter-in-law, and Bryan Jr.'s mom had gathered around him while a group of family and friends also gathered downstairs in the hospital, by faith and in support of his healing. Each day, someone would volunteer to bring food, coffee, or whatever was needed. They would ensure my husband, Lexi, and everyone there had something to eat as they waited in expectation of my son's healing. The hearts of others responded when we were weak and at our lowest point. Those relationships stepped in, surrounded us, held us up, and carried us through each day.

When I was my son's caregiver, I watched him journey through cancer like a champion, never in a spirit of defeat but always in optimism and hope. I watched him grow in strength and ring the bell. I had also listened to him when he said, "Mom, the cancer is back."

I watched Bryan Jr. dig in deep the second time around, refusing to die, having just enough strength to live. I watched him become so weak from fighting that, through FaceTime, I could only speak words of encouragement, pray, and share stories of what I was learning about digital currency. He had been teaching me about various crypto currencies and our chats about it would encourage him. I would look at him with the oxygen machine on his face and the feeding tube in his nose. I wasn't able to visit or be by his side, so seeing him through the phone from my recovery recliner brought tears to my eyes and many thoughts and questions to my mind.

I had to get rid of the guilt of not having been there with him. I had to talk myself out of being concerned what others would say when they didn't see me at the hospital. Most people didn't know about my cancer diagnosis, let alone my recent mastectomy, so they wouldn't understand why I wasn't there. I was empowered when I remembered my plan of choosing to take care of myself and also having an inner circle that supported me and knew the details of my treatment plan. Remembering my personal plan gave me permission to "be" while releasing myself from the opinions and judgments of others.

Even after overcoming thoughts of guilt and possible judgment from others, I couldn't shake the heaviness that came over me that I, the person who had been his primary caregiver, couldn't be there to hold his hand during his final moments. I had become the patient, and I needed to help myself. In some ways, it felt like a cruel joke, yet it was also humbling.

DEATH COMES NEAR

After experiencing my son's death, it felt like the dam in my mind and heart broke the levee, and an avalanche of fear broke through. My thoughts and my emotions went haywire. I couldn't hold back thoughts of my own death anymore. It was now up close and personal and required more strength than I believed I had. I couldn't shake the feeling that death had come for my son and was also coming for me. This time, death wasn't in an article online or a Facebook post. It was right in front of me, with the son I raised and cared for, the son who rang the cancer-free bell and experienced victory.

Those days after Bryan Jr.'s passing were some of the hardest days of my life. I recalled how I had wrestled with God like Jacob wrestled with the angel. For three years, I said I wasn't willing to let go until God blessed me with my son being healed. I was the lead intercessor, one who teaches others how to go before God in prayer, one who teaches others to trust God and His promises. It gutted me that my prayer had not been answered.

I had started the journey by obeying the instructions to clear my heart and go through the process of forgiveness. This forgiveness opened my heart to my son. It brought us closer than I ever imagined possible. My own cancer diagnosis in the midst of his illness had put him in the role of encourager for me. We now had a unique bond of being "port buddies." Only God could have orchestrated this bond only we shared. God drew us closer through forgiveness for all the things I didn't know would lie ahead.

As we drew closer through our car rides and nightly crypto meetings, I just knew the closeness wouldn't end. I just knew that when I prayed, it would be answered. I just knew that because we been through so much together—not through my womb but through the connection of cancer—that he would live.

The story was supposed to have a different ending. I was praying and watching the clues, but what I got was a bitter end after the sweetness of our closeness. Why would God open the door of my heart with forgiveness if He knew He was going to take my son away? Why did He cause us to get close, only to allow death to separate us?

I had done everything I believed in my heart to do, and my prayers weren't answered. My faith and my prayers couldn't stop death. I knew it was God's time, but I didn't understand it. I had drawn so much closer to God through this journey. Why didn't He grant me understanding?

Why hadn't he answered my prayers?

Why had God allowed this?

Why?

THE FINAL QUESTION

The reality of going to the church, standing in the processional line, and waiting to walk down the aisle to celebrate my son's life was surreal. It felt real, but it didn't feel real. I walked down the aisle in a sanctuary filled with more than four hundred people—death pictured around me and a fight with death within me. Every step was hard to make because I could feel the pain in my chest from grief and from surgery. The tears, emotions, and thoughts compounded my physical pain.

Even though I looked good outwardly, no one knew the physical and emotion pain I was standing in. I had decided and prepared, without thought of pain or death, to share a few words about my son to commemorate his life. To this day, I don't know if it was passion, faith, or fight that overtook me as I spoke about my son's life and his battle with cancer. As I stood to talk about him, I also encouraged myself. At my weakest, I refused to allow death to stop me or defeat me in this last moment with my son.

I was in so much pain that I was unable to hold my arms up to hug the attendees. I had to leave immediately after the funeral. Even as people asked for me, one of the individuals from my inner circle whisked me away, taking me home so I could rest. I am sure some couldn't understand why I left so abruptly. I was relieved to return home to my recovery recliner.

In that recliner, I continued to talk to God. Yes, my heart was heavy about having just buried my son. But I couldn't shake another nagging thought, even as the days and weeks passed: *Was Bryan Jr. saved?*

Weeks before Bryan Jr.'s passing, my husband asked me, "Did Bryan ever accept salvation?" The truth was, I didn't know if he had believed and accepted Jesus as Lord over his life. I remember asking Bryan Sr. if he could find an opportunity, while our son lay in the hospital bed, to pray the salvation prayer with him, if he wasn't too physically weak. The final days were so sensitive, and I didn't have the heart to ask if he'd had the chance to do it. It was too tender a time.

It was traumatizing to think of my son going through all he went through, only to have heaven not be his final resting place. I kept the uncertainty of this to myself. But my heart could not rest. I didn't have peace. For months, I wrestled with this in my mind and heart.

Almost a year after his death, I attended a women's conference. The pastor asked me to come up, and he prayed with me. As he did, he said, "You have been wondering where your son is since his death. Know that he was talking with God and he is with God!" No one but me and God knew about this lingering thought that plagued my spirit. And now, here, the God of the universe was answering my question in an unmistakable way.

I let out the biggest cry—it was as though I was giving birth! I couldn't contain the joy I felt in my being, knowing my son was at peace. Even though I still don't understand why my son's story ended this way, God has given me peace beyond my understanding. I still trust God.

YOUR TURN

Take some time to express your raw emotions about an unanswered prayer. To be able to express your raw, uncharted feelings, create a private and safe environment where you can be vulnerable. Engage in free writing to let your emotions flow without censorship or judgment.

If you are expressing uncharted feelings, allow

yourself to cry as you connect with your emotions and revisit thoughts and memories, as it's a natural and healing response. If the feelings become overwhelming, don't hesitate to seek professional support to provide you with a structured approach to navigating and articulating these deep emotions.

A Closing Prayer

Father, we are grateful for Your love, grace, and mercy. Because of Your unfailing love, we can trust and rest in You when we encounter grief. Psalm 34:18 says, "The Lord is near the broken-hearted; he saves those crushed in spirit" (CSB). Matthew 5:4 also states, "Blessed are they that mourn: for they shall be comforted" (KJV). We ask that You comfort and draw near to those who are broken, devasted, and confused by their loss. May Your love bring healing to the hearts of us who have journeyed through the loss of our loved ones, family members, and friends. Be with us in the memories and emotional ebbs and flows of grief. Although weeping may endure for a night, we declare joy will follow in the morning. May Your promises of healing, hope, and joy preserve our lives daily so we can experience brighter days in the days to come, in Jesus' name. Amen!

Chapter 9

PAIN IS A GIFT

THERE WERE DAYS I would cry, thinking about the love I received through the loss of my son. I would cry because I was so grateful. I remember one day I was confined to my recovery recliner in our bedroom. Bryan brought me dinner, which had been delivered by one of our friends. He placed the meal before me—it was from one of our favorite hibachi restaurants—and tears began to flow down my cheeks.

Before I knew it, a loud, uncontrolled wail flew out of my mouth. I was overwhelmed by God's love and the kindness of others toward my family and me.

Bryan heard me crying, and he ran back into the room to check on me. All I could say, with tears streaming down my face, was, "I am so grateful!" I knew it was hard for him to comprehend the loud, uncontrolled wail, my tears, and my words of being grateful. It was like my behavior and words didn't match. When my daughter asked him why I was crying, his response was, "She said she's grateful." LOL!

I had never experienced this form of love before. It was hard to explain how deeply the love of God and the love of others penetrated my heart. I had gotten so accustomed to giving, empowering, praying for, and encouraging others that I never sat still enough to receive. I remember thinking in those tear-filled gratitude moments, "People love me! They love me for me. They love me not for the title or what I bring, but they love me for me."

Now, looking back on that moment, I am sure grief opened my heart in such a way that gratitude found a unique form of expression I couldn't control or explain. It was a message that exploded in my heart. I guess you could say the pain delivered a gift.

> It is good for me that I have been afflicted; that I might learn thy statues.
> PSALM 119:71, KJV

> Before I was afflicted I went astray,
>   but now I keep Your word.
> PSALM 119:67, ESV

Psalm 119 says, "It is good for me that I have been afflicted." But was it? I pondered what that might mean: What if pain was gift, and I couldn't see what was inside? What if pain was a wake-up call to a more meaningful life? What if it was a wake-up call to a healthier life? What if pain was bringing me to new discoveries? What if pain was bringing me into deeper and more meaningful relationship connections?

THE GIFT OF RELATIONSHIPS

I heard it once said, "You're not wealthy if you only have money." We live a bankrupt life if we don't have or take the time to invest in heartfelt, meaningful relationships around us. Meaningful, heartfelt relationships bring love, peace, joy, support, companionship, care, gratitude, gifts, resources, access, and even money. When you invest in meaningful relationships, the return comes when you need it the most. During challenging seasons of our lives—which we all will have—those relationships will give you more than money alone can give.

Now, on the contrary, there were days I cried because I couldn't understand the pain, both physically and emotionally. The pain of losing my son. The pain of trying to understand why when I had a history of good health. Why the pain when I was just taking care of my son as a caregiver? Why the pain when I was just promoted as a pastor? Why the pain when I was faithfully teaching, empowering, serving, praying, and believing for others? Why the pain when I believed I was doing everything right but things were turning out so wrong? Why the pain when I thought I was spiritually in alignment with God and my purpose?

Pain! It didn't make sense! It was the pain of being confused. I thought I was in God's will and plan, doing what He called me to do. The truth is when you're walking through pain, especially when you don't understand, it's too excruciating for it to feel like a gift.

The pain wasn't easy to bear, but I needed to understand the reason for this season of my life. As I mentioned in an earlier chapter, this was my "Job season." Although my life paralleled this Bible character, I needed to understand more. But until I gained full understanding, I was confident in one thing: God was with me.

> "Don't be afraid, for I am with you.
>> Don't be discouraged, for I am your God.
> I will strengthen you and help you.
>> I will hold you up with my victorious right hand."
>>> —Isaiah 41:10, NLT

> "When you pass through the waters, I will be with you;
>> and through the rivers, they shall not overwhelm you;
> when you walk through fire you shall not be burned,
>> and the flame shall not consume you."
>>> —Isaiah 43:2, NRSV

The Gift of Faith

I once heard it said, "Pain is a gift that strengthens your faith." Wow—isn't this the truth? After all I had learned, developed, and shared over the years, I didn't realize my faith needed more strengthening and stretching. But did you notice in that last statement that I said, "After all *I* did"? There is something wrong with that statement. In my quiet place, I began to see the reflection of my own heart. My heart was being exposed. I was being allowed to see what I would not normally see when I was busy teaching, serving, empowering. and coaching others.

I have never wanted to accept pain as necessary. It's not a comfortable truth to accept, especially when you're facing a difficult situation and life hangs in the balance. But it was under these circumstances that I began to glimpse an understanding that pain was necessary to strengthen and stretch my faith. Sometimes God will leave us in our pain, not because He's trying to be mean but because He's trying to teach, grow, and develop a new perspective in us. I would cry and ask God why, and He would answer by leaving me in my pain.

Sounds weird, right?

Let's refer back to Isaiah 43:2 where it says, "When you pass through the waters, I will be with you; and through the rivers, they shall not overwhelm you; when you walk through fire you shall not be burned, and the flame shall not consume you." Receiving a cancer diagnosis is like being sentenced to death, and it can cause a person to give up before they even begin their fight.

Once I became quiet and began meditating on this scripture, I realized my focus shouldn't be on the cancer but on what God was doing beyond the cancer. Focusing on the cancer would only overwhelm me and cause me to drown in all it comes with. This is the opposite of the promise given in that scripture. When I read Isaiah 43:2, the promise is that I will pass through. I will pass through cancer, no matter the report of the doctor and all the tests and scans I complete.

Believing Scripture in the midst of pain increased my strength and caused me to see beyond the pain. Pain was not my limit or my end! I took this as my personal promise, and my faith shifted my focus to know that pain was stretching and strengthening me.

Emotionally and physically, there were times I felt

confused, disoriented, uncertain, and lost. This represented the waters being up to my neck. But I believed I would not drown. In the waiting period, between scans and surgeries, I felt frustrated and confused because I didn't have direction or a solid treatment plan. In the process of not knowing, I realized God was pulling me closer to Him.

Even though God didn't cause the cancer, it was allowed. Like with Job, God allowed this season to test my honor, faithfulness, and integrity toward Him. It also applied increased pressure to my faith. For me, the pressure on my faith felt like fire to the flesh. It's the pressures we face and endure in the times of adversity that demonstrate and reveal new levels of strength. Proverbs 24:10 says, "If thou faint in the day of adversity, thy strength is small" (KJV).

THE GIFT OF MORE

The pain increased my compassion to encourage others who may be walking through the cancer fight. It also had a way of driving a deep hunger in me to want to learn more about what I was facing. I gained more knowledge about my enemy, cancer. I discovered more about myself and gained an appetite for the mindset and mysteries of God.

When you read Job 1:7–22, notice the Lord gave Satan permission to test Job for the purposes of wisdom and faith in order to strengthen and advance the plans of God. God's permission was designed to display God's power and character through Job. When we read further into the remaining verses, we see Job lose his farm animals, his servants, and his children as a result of this permission. God wasn't only testing Job emotionally and physically, but also spiritually, to display the character of his heart. The heart is known to be deceitful and can turn its back on God in any situation. Job's strength, wisdom, courage, confidence, and obedience to God resided in his heart. This was God's true purpose when He chose Job for this test.

When going through adversity, it is important to get quiet. Getting quiet and silencing the voices, opinions, and expectations of others allowed me to hear God's voice and His instructions. We are unique, and so are the adversity and challenges we all go through. Even though a diagnosis sounds the same for many people, the process will be different for each person—hence, the reason it's important to be still and know.

In my still moments, I gave myself the opportunity to filter and process my experience through the Word and mindset of God. In my still moments with God, I couldn't help but think that, like Job, God gave Satan permission to test me. What if this had nothing to do with cancer but was more about the character, commitment, capacity, and courage I would need for my future?

The story of Job didn't take away the pain, but it gave me parallel I could understand and relate to. For example, Job was afflicted with painful sores from his head to his toes (Job 2:7). I am sure he felt severe pain, and I could relate to that.

I didn't lose livestock like Job did, but this cancer diagnosis did attack my finances. It felt like cancer came with a vengeance to swallow up my finances because of all the initial doctor appointments that were needed before I secured health insurance. I also knew how much cancer could cost because of the expenses my son incurred during his treatments. Almost immediately, my co-payments and hospital balances became a permanent part of our monthly expenses.

And then, just like Job lost his children, I watched my son take his last breath on March 16, 2022. There were so many reasons to cry, cry, and cry some more. But as I filtered my emotions through the promises of God, He ministered to me and encouraged me with His Word, reminding me, "I will be with you!"

As the scripture said, it felt like I had passed through the fire—and sometimes it felt like that happened literally. After having a double mastectomy surgery, with lots of lymph nodes removed and nerves compromised, I can remember nights when the pain did feel like fire, and there was nothing to cool it down. I would cry and sing quietly to myself and to the Lord.

I felt a fire in my body, but I also felt a fire within my heart—a fire that illuminated and removed things I couldn't see. As God healed me, He also cleaned up and purged my heart and character. Pain slowed me down to see those things I couldn't see when I was busy doing life, parenting, ministry, marriage, and business. It's interesting how much I could clearly hear myself and see my behavior and attitude when I was still. God used this momentary place of affliction to do a work in my heart to make room for more grace, mercy, peace, compassion, fervency, forgiveness, and more.

When pain is present and we pray and cry for relief,

we expect God to let us off the hook. Though the pain is legitimate, we may not always get an automatic pass from God simply because we cry out. I believe God doesn't let us off the hook or feel sorry for us in the face of adversity because He knows the impact of our purpose and potential on a higher scale than we do. Although God loves me, He didn't feel sorry for me, and that's because of the potential that was within me and the greater purpose that would come after this.

God is seeing us, teaching us, encouraging us, and coaching us from the place of our strength. He not only responds to the pain, but He speaks to the potential of who we are becoming. Once I realigned my thoughts, focusing on how God uses pain for the benefit of revealing and developing my strength, I began to align with the new thing He was doing within me.

The pain of affliction was necessary to push and squeeze out any ungodly character in me. Through it, my mental, emotional, and spiritual capacity was stretched and enlarged. God allowed me to walk through this fiery affliction to remove and detach me from my doubts, ambition, fears, pride, people approval, and impatience. What's interesting about this is that the walking through is real! Like the scripture said, when you walk through the fire, you will not be burned and the flames shall not consume you. It took me more than five hundred days to walk through and grow in strength. Pain is a gift.

DON'T WASTE THE PAIN

Though pain is a gift, some people avoid receiving it. Unprocessed pain can produce and increase a person's anger, bitterness, resentment, doubt, stress, and fear. Pain can incite lies and uncertainty for the purpose of muzzling the truth. It can harden the heart and bring division within a person. Pain can cause a person to give up on their faith, future, and purpose. It can cause a person to give up on God, only to go another way. Pain can turn a person into an addict, making their only mission to remain numb and disconnected by indulging in poor eating habits, drugs, alcohol, sex, and spending. Pain can slowly lead a person into depression, isolation, and hopelessness.

Pain is a gift, and the only way out is through faith. It is believing God that there is more beyond this adversity, this sickness, this situation, and this season. We read in Matthew 6:33, "Seek the Kingdom of God above all else, and live righteously, and he will give you everything you need" (NLT). For me, this means when I seek God consistently, He will give me the understanding I need. I have learned not to give my emotions permission to interpret or determine my outcome, direction, or results. When I gain understanding through faith, it gives me an inner peace.

Unraveling the pain with the promises and principles of God repositioned my mind and heart to think and believe with hope. I repositioned myself from patient to student. Being a patient would put me at the mercy of my doctors. However, being a student put me in position to learn more about God as my healer, teacher, provider, lifter, and the truth. The student becomes eager and patient, not just for healing but also to learn.

Pain is a gift. God doesn't want to waste the pain.

God wants to redeem our suffering. You can always help and encourage more people through your weaknesses than your strengths. Sharing and talking about all things good won't help someone in their pain. However, sharing with a person who is walking through a painful season how God walked you through your painful season could empower and change their life.

I would never have thought in a million years that I would ever share one of the biggest pains of my life—losing my son and simultaneously being diagnosed with cancer. I didn't have time to catch my breath. I had to grieve and heal at the same time. I didn't ask for this ministry. I didn't think this was going to be a part of my purpose and plan. But I know that as a result of this journey, God will allow me to bring hope and healing to women who have walked through breast cancer, grief, the loss of a child, issues with body image, and so much more.

I remember receiving a text from someone asking for prayer for her niece who had recently been diagnosed with breast cancer. The text described the details of her situation, and my heart immediately filled with compassion because it reflected my situation and story. I said to myself, tears streaming down my face, "She is me, and I am her!" I knew how to pray for her immediately because I knew what some of her thoughts, concerns, fears, doubts, and decisions would be.

I believe pain is a gift. I have become a "safe place" for women to find comfort, connection, confidence, peace, strength, and empowerment. Being in the trenches of pain and rising from it allows me to give others that same strength—and even greater. Pain becomes a gift when you endure through the process and do not prematurely pull out.

Pain, often perceived as an unwelcome intruder, is paradoxically a gift in its own right because it arrives cloaked in discomfort. My yes to seeing pain as a gift gave me access to profound teaching and transformation. My yes to pain gifted me with a deeper understanding of my resilience. It gifted me with an increased capacity to endure, a heightened awareness of this journey, a clearer vision of what truly matters, and the strength I never knew I had. My yes was a gift that pushed me beyond my "pain tolerance" to discover the boundless potential I possess within.

YOUR TURN

A part of God's plan for our lives is that we help others, not just through our gifts, accomplishments, and resources, but also through the encouragement that is birthed in our pain. Pain is a gift!

- Recall a time when pain blinded you to seeing beyond where you were. How did you work through the feelings of defeat?

- How has going through cancer or a health crisis made you stronger or more resilient?

- Can you recall a painful moment that eventually led to personal growth or success?

- In what ways has pain shaped your perspective on life's challenges? What lessons or gifts have you received from enduring pain that you wouldn't have realized otherwise?

- How has God used your pain to minister to others facing the same trial?

A Closing Prayer

Father, we confess that cancer brings pain physically, emotionally, mentally, and financially. When pain comes to cause us to lose our hope and direction, we put our trust in You. Your Word says in Isaiah 43:2, "When you pass through the waters, I will be with you; and when you pass through the rivers, they will not sweep over you. When you walk through the fire, you will not be burned; the flames will not set you ablaze" (NIV). We thank You that You have given us the promise that You will be with us in the pain. We thank You that with You, pain becomes a gift of resilience, strength, growth, endurance, value, and increased faith. We thank You that the gift of pain allows us to connect with who and what matters the most. We thank You and praise You in Jesus' name. Amen!

Chapter 10

THE DEATH OF ME

FTER BURYING MY son, I realized this was just the first level of dealing with death. The day after the funeral, I was scheduled for an appointment with my oncologist to discuss the findings of a bronchoscopy, where they inserted a scope into my mouth to view my lungs. This meeting was to determine the type of treatment plan I needed so we could eradicate this disease.

The oncologist informed me the procedure was inconclusive and that I would need to have a thoracic lung biopsy. This time, they would insert a needle in the chest cavity. Because of this, my treatment plan would once again be placed on hold. We could not move forward until we learned the findings of this procedure.

Immediately, I felt the emotional turbulence hit me again. I felt a drop in my stomach. My mind was prepared and set to move forward and begin treatment so I could get back on track with my life. This delay brought another level of frustration, fear, and impatience. I felt they knew something but weren't telling me, that my doctor was holding out on me, and that the world around me was moving on and leaving me behind. Tears, fear, and frustration welled up within me. The fear of seeing a thoracic surgeon created the worst image of them cutting me open. Fear, impatience, and doubt took its free course with me.

After talking it out with my inner circle and taking a few days to process and pray, I realized the root of my fear was my impatience. I was impatient to know the outcome of the treatment plan. I was impatient to get back on track with my life because I had been sitting out for four months. I was impatient with the doctors, thinking they already knew what was going on and were keeping me in the dark. I was impatient because I wanted to help bring finances into our home through my business to relieve some of the financial pressure on our family. I was impatient with God by not trusting Him.

Impatience was the culprit driving my fears that sparked the thoughts of death. Impatience tried to put me in control, when in all actuality, I was not in control. Impatience created unnecessary frustration and disappointment, which facilitated a bunch of stories in my head that weren't true. I allowed impatience to fight the plan and process. Impatience caused me to get in the way. I wanted to get on with my life and my scheduled plan. Impatience pushed my agenda and moved me away from God's agenda. It moved me out of my position of peace and into accepting pressure.

In this moment, I realized the problem wasn't the doctors or God. It was me. I had to do some work with my impatience. I could feel the nudge of God's voice, saying, "Have I called you to return to your scheduled duties? What are you rushing back to do? Whose time-table are you on, yours or Mine? Who holds the final plan, you or Me?" As these questions fired off at me, I could feel myself slowly move out of fear and into truth. I started to get out of God's way.

I will admit I had never been still this long. This was new for me. Though I knew being sidelined had a purpose—to care for myself, heal, and get rest—it was difficult. My only responsibility was self-care, while I allowed God, my family, and my friends to take care of me.

But I was desperately impatient. And I felt justified in my worry, anxiety, and impatience. I had just buried my son and knew the importance of attacking cancer as early as possible. I felt the longer we waited without treatment, the more opportunity cancer had to spread in my body. I didn't know where that cancer was going, and I wanted to stop it.

But then God, as He ministered to me in my recovery recliner, began to show me that through this process, I would die to the nature of who I once was. I would die to my ways, my habits, my desires, my ambition, my reputation, my fears, and my attitude to come alive in a higher form of existence through faith.

From Death to Life

Death produces life. Remember that earlier passage from John 12:24? It says, "I tell you the truth, unless a kernel of wheat is planted in the soil and dies, it remains alone. But its death will produce many new kernels—a plentiful harvest of new lives" (NLT). This verse refers to a spiritual death. Cancer is known to kill, but my focus would not be on the cancer. I would focus instead on dying to self. The cancer decomposes, but I would come alive in the principles of God. I would come alive to share, pray, and empower others to live in spite of cancer. This would harvest plenty more new lives, so they too could experience hope.

Anytime something dies, a transformation takes place. My mind, heart, and vision were being transformed to focus on the process within instead of the outcome. In the transformation from death to life, I am not in control of the process. Hence, the reason God posed the question to me: "Are you in control of the plan?" Impatience pushed me to get ahead, which would cause me to miss the changes taking place within me.

When we live without God, we're unable to endure, live, and produce more in hard times and challenges. When we partner with God, He wants to get the glory out of our lives so others can see He is who He says He is. Therefore, God has a vested interest in us being triumphant. His name is on the line when we work together! I yielded based on this new level of insight.

A Surrendered Peace

When the thoracic surgeon contacted me, he explained the procedure and the healing process. He was insightful and patient over the phone. I thought they were going to stick a huge needle in my back or cut open my chest to get to my lungs. That was not the procedure at all, he explained. We talked through the details, and I had a measure of peace. Once I yielded to God's plan, not impatience and fear, peace took over and things began to line up. Peace paved the way to understanding.

I returned to God's instruction, promise, and plan noted in Psalm 23 and created another personal prayer of His promises.

> God is my Good Shepherd!
> I have everything I need; I lack nothing.
> He supplies all of my needs.
> I rest in His truth and promises.
> I allow His grace to be my portion as He guides
> me in peace and directs my path.
> He will give me strength for the journey.
> He will guide me along the right path.
> In the shadow of death, I don't stop. I keep going,
> and I pass through with courage.
> He goes before me; with Him before me, nothing
> can stand against me,
> for I am fearlessly and wonderfully made.
> He didn't give me the spirit of fear, but He gave
> me His love, power, and a sound mind.
> I will work daily and diligently to study, build,
> improve, maintain, and sustain my sound
> mind.
> Always remember, God is with me on the
> journey.
> He will protect and comfort me.
> On this journey, God will prepare a table before
> me in the presence of my enemies.
> For my endurance, obedience, and steadfastness,
> God anoints my head with oil.
> My cup runs over with blessings—blessings of
> health, wisdom, wealth, favor, and strength.

> Goodness and mercy will follow me all the days
> of my life, and I will forever dwell in the
> house of the Lord. Amen!

Because I chose to believe and trust God, I now surrender even more. To surrender means to willfully and completely give up my own will, ideas, and thoughts to align with God's plan. To surrender means accepting that battles are won when they are given over to the authority of the unfailing winning team. It means taking a humble position and embracing the process in obedience. To surrender is to let go of the control to trust God. Sometimes our mouth says we are willing to surrender until an experience or situation exposes our true will.

I had a trust issue. Did I trust God with my life? Could I let go of control to trust God? This was the hardest part of the process. It becomes hard because it is a decisive blow against my flesh. Galatians 2:20 says, "I have been crucified with Christ; it is no longer I who live, but Christ lives in me; and the life which I now live in the flesh I live by faith in the Son of God, who loved me and gave Himself for me" (NIV). When Christ was facing death, He too had to surrender. Christ gave up His will to align with the Father's plan. When Christ followed the Father's plan, He received victory over death through the resurrection. I surrender not to the fear or threat of death but in hope that God has a better life for me after this.

To know what areas I needed to surrender, I went to God in prayer. Once revealed, I wrote them down on paper so I would become more aware of it in my behaviors. Below are my surrender points that helped clear the path to gain power over death.

- I surrender to knowing I don't know everything, but through faith, I can have what I believe.

- I surrender to not knowing where this is leading, but with God, His plans are to prosper me and not harm me, plans to give me a hope and a future.

- I surrender to the fact that God is the Light; as I travel through this shadow of darkness, He will illuminate my path with instructions and directions.

- I surrender my thoughts, my plans, my agenda, my emotions, my experience, my intellect, my fears, and my doubts because they limit my freedom and distort my vision.

- I surrender my old mindset to make room for a fresh, new perspective on my situation and to gain wisdom.

- I surrender my imperfections so God can perfect, establish, strengthen, and settle me in this battle, like a tree that is planted and can't be uprooted.

- I surrender my doubts and worries,
  believing miracles and healing are more
  than possible through my life.

- I surrender my doubts, while believing
  signs, miracles, and wonders will follow
  me.

MY TREATMENT PLAN

Three weeks after the biopsy procedure, I had an appointment with my oncologist to review the report of the thoracic surgeon and find out the treatment results. Bryan and I walked into the examination room, and the nurse took my vitals. Then we waited for the doctor to come in. While we waited, Bryan reviewed emails for his job and I listened to a sermon on my phone.

The doctor walked in with my file. He pulled the stool toward him with his foot and sat down. Then he pulled up the computer images on screen. "We finally have results," he said. "The report from the thoracic surgeon says the cancer has spread to the lungs. The spots are very small, but we still want to treat them. Your diagnosis is now stage 4 metastatic breast cancer."

I reached for Bryan's hand because the words *stage 4* brought me back to my son's experience. My mind raced and my heart started beating fast. Just a few weeks prior, I had buried my son, whose cancer had rapidly spread from his lungs to his heart and up into his brain in a matter of weeks. My anxiety rose, and I started crying.

"Your story is not his story," the doctor said, sensing what this news of stage 4 was doing in my mind. He explained that although the spots were few and small in nature, it was categorized as stage 4 because it had gone from the breast to the lungs.

"Where do we go from here?" I asked.

"At this point, we will not treat with chemotherapy and radiation as previously discussed. Instead, we will do a hormone treatment," he said. "There are great medications now on the market that will work."

I thought back to the story Varian had shared with me about the treatment her mom had been given. The oncologist told me the side effects would be a bit hard on the body. However, they had a plan to help manage those. Every month, I would have lab appointments, and every quarter, we would continue with the scans to monitor my progress.

Even though this gift came packaged in a stage 4 diagnosis, I saw it as another gift from God that I would not have to endure chemotherapy and radiation.

God answered my prayers by turning the proposed treatment plan around in my favor. Even though stage 4 metastatic breast cancer sounds bad—and it is—it was the plan God suited for me. I gave my yes to dying to my old mindset, which opened my eyes to see what I couldn't see while consumed with my fears, doubts, and impatience. Because of that, I could see this plan had already been scripted for my victory. This was the plan that would minister to and most effectively be a witness to many. This was the plan that aligned with my purpose and passion. I was thankful for God's mercy and grace while I was bearing the unbearable.

Through this journey, I called upon God's name, and

this was a sign of His faithfulness. He was delivering me from having chemotherapy and radiation. Because of His faithfulness toward me, I would honor Him.

YOUR TURN

Life is subject to change. When you have faith in God, it helps you to see beyond the cancer and health condition. Traveling through a health condition is almost never a straight line to victory; it is riddled with unexpected ups, downs, and turns. Having faith during these times of change serves as a crucial anchor, providing stability and comfort amidst uncertainty. It encourages individuals to embrace the unknown with a sense of peace, trusting there is a larger plan or purpose beyond their immediate understanding. Faith offers guidance through its teachings, which can be applied to navigate life's transitions more gracefully. Although we expect victory through our faith, the process invites us into greater levels of surrender. Consistent obedience in faith helps us maintain a grounded perspective, patience, peace, and gratitude. Ultimately, faith instills hope and reassurance, reminding us we are not alone in our journey when life inevitably changes.

- What is your immediate emotional response to unexpected life changes?

- Make a list of emotions that stand in your way of having a clear mind during adversity.

- Choose one of the emotions you listed above. Which one of God's promises will you take hold of as you let go of that negative emotion?

- What benefits do you anticipate having as you surrender?

A CLOSING PRAYER

Father, 1 Thessalonians 5:16–18 says, "Let joy be your continual feast. Make your life a prayer. And in the midst of everything be always giving thanks, for this is God's perfect plan for you" (TPT). Today, we give thanks in the up and down times of life. We surrender our will, emotions, understanding, and expectations to hold steadfast in our faith and trust in You. Clear the path of our hearts and minds, that we can see through the lens of hope. Help us navigate the challenges of life with Your peace, guidance, insight, and wisdom. We ask that not only do You heal us but transform us to become a better version of who we are. May our faith in You instill confidence and reassurance, reminding us You are with us. In Jesus' name, amen!

Chapter 11

THE SUMMIT

I AM NOT A friend of heights. When I confront heights, my pulse races with visceral terror. Dizziness threatens to overwhelm me, and I'm so sure I can feel the ground beneath me sway. The heights make my head swim with vertigo, and each glance down sends shivers of petrifying fear through my veins. My stomach churns with a nauseating cocktail of dread and anxiety, each downward glance amplifying the fear that clutches at my throat. My palms get slippery with cold sweat, and I struggle to maintain a grip on anything solid. My breaths come in short, sharp gasps as thinner air claws at my lungs, heightening a suffocating panic. The vast expanse of space below me seems to invite an intensifying, paralyzing sense of vulnerability. Even as I stand immobilized, a silent battle rages within between the instinctive urge to flee from the dizzying precipice and the rational part of my mind that strives to calm the storm of panicky apprehension. The feeling of dread I feel when at uncomfortable heights comes close to what I imagine it would be like to climb a mountain in the Alps!

On one our movie nights, Bryan selected the movie

The Alpinist. Even though I'd seen it before, I agreed to watch it again. This movie is a documentary about a young, twenty-three-year-old unknown mountain climber, Marc-André Leclerc, who had a passion for climbing ginormous mountains. Since I'd watched the documentary before and knew how it would end, my attention to the movie shifted this time.

This time I watched it as though I was in the shoes of the young climber. When I did that, I recognized so many similarities between the mountains he had a passion for climbing and the mountain of sickness I faced. I won't narrate the entire documentary, but I encourage you to watch it when you face insurmountable seasons or challenges that seem greater than you. It's a great reminder not to look at the mountain but at what you gain on the climb!

An alpinist is a climber of steep, high mountains, especially the Alps mountain ranges in Europe. From the documentary, I learned so much about a climber's mindset when they approach and stand in front of a seemingly insurmountable, larger-than-life mountain. For example, when Marc-André approached four thousand feet of mixed terrain of ice and rock, he didn't allow the size of the mountain or the terrain to stir up any doubt or intimidation. He had more confidence in his training and his abilities than in its appearance or the fate of other climbers. His confidence and mental capacity developed by climbing mountain after mountain. He approached each mountain with passion, ability, skill, grace, confidence, courage, and determination.

His confidence was so unwavering that you couldn't tell him he couldn't climb that mountain.

Marc-André practiced free climbing, which means no rope, no parachute, and no safety harness. This was evidence of his fearlessness and determination. Without those safety devices, his senses heightened to listen to the direction of the wind, feel the heat and direction of the sun, hear the sound of melting ice and loose rock, and hear the ice pick hook into the ice or mountain. Even if he began with a preliminary plan, he improvised once he began a climb, adjusting to and being guided by the mountain.

It was interesting to hear him say he climbed each mountain knowing death was a factor. If death wasn't present with the climb, what would be the point? Because he knew he risked death, the climb became more adventurous and made him feel more alive.

Now let's think about us. How many mountains do we face in life? There are certainly mountains that seem bigger than us and almost insurmountable to climb. Would you still give your yes to climbing a major mountain in life, even if death was a possibility?

Well, my answer is yes!

But unlike Marc-André, this was my first time trying to climb a mountain of this size. When we face a mountainous life challenge, it is not easy to stand in front of it and scale it with confidence and grace. Even though I had scaled previous challenges, they were nothing like the size of this one, where I had lost my son and was also facing my diagnosis. This mountain made past challenges look like hills. However, conquering smaller-sized mountains had prepared me for this bigger mountain.

I saw similarities between Marc-André's experience as an alpinist and my experience of navigating this mountain called cancer. For example, even though I had a preliminary plan as I approached this cancer mountain, I also had to improvise and be guided by the Holy Spirit. Then there's the fact that he climbed solo. He didn't have a lot of people with him so he could remain focused and become sensitive to the sound of nature. Similarly, I wanted to be alone to be alert to the voice of God. He climbed with no rope or safety device and believed in himself. I had only my faith and trust in God to conquer this mountain. And like Marc, I had a determination to endure and conquer.

Every time Marc climbed mountains, he knew death was a factor. Likewise, my cancer mountain came with an automatic death sentence, and I refused to surrender to it. Marc described the adventurous journey as one where he was his "freest." also too, can say that although this journey has been my most challenging, it has also been my most liberating. In order for me to make a steady climb, I had to pack light. This meant detaching myself from roles, responsibilities, relationships, titles, ambition, accolades, opinions, expectations, image, and time—and leaving them behind.

LET'S TALK TOOLS

My tools were a bit different than Marc-André's. To be successful on his climb, he carried light weather gear, a tent that folded as a backpack, climbing shoes with spikes, a helmet with a headlight, gloves, two metal climbing pics, metal clips, a communication device, and light snacks. These tools were selected to prepare and protect him against inclement weather, avalanches, and the like.

The tools for my climb, or spiritual ascent, were a little different. I am naturally afraid of heights, so I knew how important it would be to keep my focus. Just like I would do on an actual mountain, I needed to not look down or turn around to go back down the mountain. Looking beyond death and cancer took tremendous focus and tremendous faith. I had to engage my faith to climb higher than what was visible to my natural eyes. To ascend spiritually, I had to block out thoughts, pain, and people to climb higher and draw closer to God. It felt like the higher I climbed, the more insight and revelation I received, which began to erode and override my fears.

Like Marc-André, I had gear. Namely, I applied the armor of God. This is the gear God provides for us to fight battles, as referenced in Ephesians 6:10–18. The armor of God is our spiritual armor.

It came to me one day. Would I ever leave my house with no clothes on to go grocery shopping, to church, or to a client meeting? Heck no! Why wouldn't I do that? Because I would be exposed and vulnerable to people and the elements around me. I would start from a defeated stance. The same concept holds true spiritually. So many things contend for our attention daily, we must remain aware so we are not distracted or destroyed by our choices.

For me, putting on the armor of God daily—and sometimes twice a day—became my routine for getting dressed spiritually. After taking a shower, I would apply the armor of God before putting on my clothes. This meant recognizing each piece of the armor and praying that piece over the body.

First, I would motion with my hands and apply the belt of truth around my waist, believing the unchanging truth about God and His promises. Then I would motion with my hands to apply the breastplate of righteousness to my chest area. The breastplate covers and protects the heart and body and would prevent me from succumbing to my fleshly choices and decisions that would weaken me. It allowed me to stand in confidence, affirming God's standard in my life so my thoughts and behaviors aligned.

I would motion with my hands and cover my feet, applying the shoes of peace that made me calm as I moved in life's mixed terrain. The shoes of peace have spikes on the bottom that help you grip the mountain and stay steady in the promises and principles of God.

I continued dressing with the shield of faith, motioning my left hand to hold the shield, which protected me from negative voices and accusations of others. The shield of faith is confidence in God's Word. It's believing God's Word so much that we act in response to His Word over our lives.

Next was the helmet of salvation, which I put on by moving my hands as if putting a helmet on my head.

This provided me with a whole new way of thinking that produced freedom and protection. Salvation is designed to reorient our identity and implement a new way of thinking by accepting Jesus Christ, who died for our sins. Salvation protects our mind and how we see ourselves so we can move successfully into our future.

Next I held the sword of the Spirit in my right hand, wielded as an offensive weapon that signaled I had everything I needed to protect myself against the schemes of the enemy.

Finally, I ended this exercise by praying in the Spirit while wearing the various pieces of armor. Praying in the Spirit is praying in your heavenly language. This maintained my focus, vision, strength, peace, and hope.

Some may say, "It doesn't take all of that to climb the mountain of a cancer diagnosis," but for me, it did. I climbed that mountain for more than five hundred days, and "all of that" helped me gain understanding, draw closer to God, hear God's voice at a higher level, understand myself outside of others, see my potential, conquer the fear of death and heights, surrender my plans, see and experience the pains and joys of others, understand and know I could count each step as joy, experience greater dimensions of faith, and—best of all—capture new views.

To Move or to Climb

Like Marc-André, I found the best feeling of success was not just conquering the mountain but seeing the views at the next level. ～～✿ The world looks different when you climb and ascend to new heights and higher dimensions!

This is why it is important to know some mountains aren't designed to crumble or move out of the way but to climb so you can experience yourself, God, and life at higher heights and deeper dimensions. At the top, you will experience a new version of yourself—a version with new potential and new strength.

All of which is to say: some mountains you move, but some mountains you must climb! The mountains we move are the ones that interfere with our morality and impede our decisions, restrict our growth and purpose, and undermine our identity. These mountains rise in the heart and can't always be seen. They're mountains of guilt, of judgment, of corruption, of rebellion, of pride. They stand in the way of our belief and cause us to second-guess ourselves. They're the ones Jesus talked about when He said:

> "I tell you the truth, you can say to this mountain, 'May you be lifted up and thrown into the sea,' and it will happen. But you must really believe it will happen and have no doubt in your heart."
> —MARK 11:23, NLT

Then there are the mountains we climb. Contrary to the ones we move, the mountains we climb are the ones that bring an invitation to spend time in the presence of God to learn more of His attributes face-to-face. This is like the mountain Moses climbed:

> Then Moses disappeared into the cloud as he
> climbed higher up the mountain. He remained on
> the mountain forty days and forty nights.
>
> —Exodus 24:18, NLT

Moses was chosen by God to lead God's people to the land of Canaan. God selected Moses for this task of leadership despite the many excuses he gave not to go. When you read the story, you see Moses encountered opposition from Pharoah several times, coupled with negative complaints and frustration from the people he led. Despite all he faced and his own frustrations, Moses stayed faithful toward God. He followed God's instructions about dealing with Pharaoh and the people.

In the end, Moses was selected by the people and instructed by God to climb the mountain, where he went up to Mount Sinai twice with God for forty days and nights each time. Within those eighty days, Moses experienced an intimacy with God no one else had experienced. He traveled through all of his personal insecurities, personal frustrations, the oppositions of Pharaoh, and the complaints of others to be rewarded with an intimate space with God.

In my case, climbing my cancer mountain transformed my life forever. The more I climbed, the greater the view and the deeper and wider my compassion for those walking through cancer and other terminal diseases. My compassion grew for caregivers, siblings, and spouses. My anger grew against cancer for the physical, emotional, mental, and financial burden it places on individuals. Just maybe, God knew I would give my yes so He could bring me through the valley of cancer, up a mountain, and away from others to experience the reward of intimacy with Him too.

Your Turn

We learn different insights, disciplines, and strategies when we climb mountains rather than move them. It's easy to think hard things like a health challenge or financial loss is a good reason to give up, but things like this can position you to climb and go higher, depending on your humility to learn and your hunger to conquer.

- What mountain are you facing that requires you to climb rather than pray for it to move?

- What does conquering this mountain mean to you?

- What is the root of your fear or hesitation when it comes to conquering your mountain?

- What steps can you take to prepare mentally, emotionally, physically, and spiritually for this ascent?

- What resources and tools do you have to help you conquer this obstacle?

- How can you maintain your motivation and focus as the climb gets tough?

A Closing Prayer

Father, we give You thanks for another day of life everlasting in You. When we face the vicissitudes and mountains of life, we recognize we need Your help. When a cancer diagnosis or other health conditions grip us with petrifying fear, terror, anxiety, and apprehension, we reach for Your hand of strength. When we feel immobilized in fear and unsure of our steps, we trust in You. We ask that You prepare us mentally, physically, emotionally, and spiritually for the climb. When the mountain stands in our way and takes us to uncomfortable heights, we don't look back but climb to draw closer to You. Provide us with the necessary tools and resources needed. We climb the mountain to hear Your voice, recognize our strength, see our potential, and grow in new dimensions of faith. We climb the mountain to ascend and capture a new view of our future. We climb the mountain to view a new perspective of our purpose. Thank You for the many insights, lessons, and possibilities that shape us and sharpen us for our future, in Jesus' name. Amen!

Chapter 12

EMERGING

PICTURE A LITTLE caterpillar with a big appetite, munching away on green goodies in the sunshine. This tiny creature is decked out in bright stripes or spots, like a moving piece of art. When it has gotten its fill, the caterpillar wraps itself up in a cozy chrysalis like it's snuggled in a sleeping bag hanging from a branch. Inside this snug hideout, something amazing happens: the caterpillar begins to change! By the next day, this once-wiggly caterpillar begins to transform.

Suddenly, a crack appears, and through this tiny opening, glimpses of brilliant colors peek out. The caterpillar inside the chrysalis is slowly turning into a butterfly. It's out with the old and in with the new as it grows wings—wings folded up like delicate origami masterpieces, waiting to be unveiled. Out comes a pair of wet, crinkled wings splashed with vibrant hues and patterns. There are dots like sapphires, stripes like ribbons of sunlight, and patches that shimmer like emeralds.

As the butterfly hangs on to its former home, it patiently waits. The wings slowly spread out, drying in the warm air. The colors become even more dazzling as they unfold, revealing a living tapestry of reds, yellows, blues, and greens that sparkle in the daylight.

With a gentle flutter, the butterfly tests its new wings. As they flap, the colors dance and blend like a painter's brush strokes on a canvas. Now fully open, the wings are a masterpiece, ready to carry the butterfly on its first flight, emerging into the bright world beyond.

The Cocoon I Knew

My journey to breast reconstruction took a year. Every three weeks after the mastectomy surgery, I went in for saline injections to fill the expander sites. Those visits were painfully uncomfortable. When the day for reconstruction finally came, I prepared myself for an extended time in my recovery recliner. Thankfully, the recovery and healing process from this reconstruction surgery was much easier than the mastectomy.

I was nervously excited about this surgery. I knew God was leading me to the end of this part of the journey and preparing me for what was to come. Even though I could feel the end near in my heart, it felt bittersweet—sweet in the sense that I had made it through, but bitter because I didn't want to give up the personal encounters I'd experienced with God. Knowing God and remembering His loving words and promises is what had gotten me through this painful journey. I had experienced grief and many losses, including my breasts, but I had captured a deeper understanding of love for myself, a deeper understanding of God's love for me, and a deeper appreciation for life. I didn't want to let go of that sweet spot I had with God.

I had spent five hundred days in a cocoon of sorts, hearing only from God and the people in my inner circle. I had no choir singing for me or creating an atmosphere of worship. No pastor to empower me daily to stir my faith. No microphone to empower others. No sound of accolades or encouragement from others. No one calling me by a title. It was silent, and the silence was even noisy at times.

The silence could have been deafening, but instead, I made it golden by creating my own atmosphere. I was able to read God's Word more intensely as I contended for my victory. I prayed fervently and listened to sermons that spoke to my condition, my state of mind, and the potential of God's power within me. The silence became golden because it illuminated and strengthened my hope. The Word of God ministered to and filled my heart with revelation and insight. I would sing and create my own songs of praise and dance passionately as God's faithful promises filled my heart. Silence was necessary for me to grow beyond the noise of the diagnosis and fill my room with praise, dance, prayer, and His promises.

In no small way, this journey reset my life. It reset my identity. God was not only transforming me from within, but also resetting how I saw myself physically and spiritually. After having a double mastectomy, it took some time for me to adjust to seeing myself with scars, without breasts, and with implants. Resetting my identity began with seeing my heart, not just the image I saw in the mirror. Resetting my identity as a woman was knowing that having breasts wasn't the essence of my beauty and that my identity and beauty are not solely connected to my physical appearance. My heart is also part of my identity and beauty. In my heart is where my strength, grace, endurance, power, passion, potential, and wisdom are found. Whether looking at myself in pictures or with clothes on or off, the reset of my identity is no longer on the surface but deep within my heart.

I believe the amount of days I spent in this cocoon was crucial to reinforce God's principles in my heart and mind. Although the journey was filled with pain and grief, it was the pain that led me to the principles. The principles brought so much insight and freedom that I made a commitment to remember what I had learned. One day, while reading Psalm 103:2 with tears streaming down my face (it says, "May I never forget the good things he does for me," NLT), I knew I didn't want to forget what He taught me, revealed to me, healed in me, graced over me, protected for me, provided for me, and comforted in me. I now wake up each morning grateful and asking God to keep me in remembrance of His principles and all He has done for me.

I want to stay humble, even in the victory. To this day, my nerve pain reminds me of what God has brought me through. It remains close to my heart and is reinforced in my thoughts, actions, and expression. I went through too much during those five hundred days to forget or waste what I learned. This journey has transformed me in such a way that I cannot forget.

THE SILENT DAYS

It's not easy or comfortable being alone for five hundred days. Even though I was surrounded by my family and inner circle, I was still alone in my thoughts, my experiences, and my feelings. My family and inner circle could only provide support to a certain point. Some questions they couldn't answer, some feelings they couldn't understand, and some thoughts they couldn't explain. I believe God made it that way.

God designed the silent days so I would be still and know He is God. In the silent days, God's voice became clearer. In the silent days, I learned to trust God's voice over other voices. In the silent days, I learned to sing and dance to my own worship songs and to release the pressure of the process. In the silent days, nothing else mattered more than my health and living. In the silent days, I silenced the stressors of life. In the silent days, I silenced the opinions and expectations of people. In the silent days, I silenced the lies of death by believing the value of my purpose and what my life brings to the world.

What I learned in the silent days prepared me to walk back into a noisy world. You see, all the bills, the demands of world, and the expectations of others—I now know how to silence it. The power of silence prevents it from overwhelming me or creating stress. If I didn't allow it to bother me when I was in my silent days, then I could refuse to allow it to bother me after my emergence!

Since coming out of my protective cocoon, I've

returned to regularly scheduled life responsibilities, such as car troubles, college tuition payments, mortgage insurance, and other bills. This can create lots of stress. But because of what I learned in the silent days, my health and my relationship with God matters most. I refuse to allow life stressors to take the life that I fought for.

Unexpected Provision

Remember how my biggest concern after the cancer diagnosis was finances? I worried the bills would drain us financially, especially because I didn't have insurance.

One day, while making breakfast for my son, he mentioned I had a critical care accelerated benefit policy and could put in a claim for the breast cancer diagnosis. He knew this because he had sold it to us and helped my husband set it up. On that same day, we called and they emailed the ten-page application, asking for detailed information regarding the diagnosis, doctor visits, specialist visits, treatment plan, and the like. For weeks, I got letters in the mail saying they needed more information, and the application was still under review.

But then Bryan Jr. died. In that haze, I remembered I hadn't heard from them in over two months, and the medical bills had started piling up. I nervously called the claim representative and asked for an update. She indicated my application had been approved on March 16 and that I would be getting a letter in the mail. She also said she would send an email with a copy of the letter. When I reviewed it and saw the amount, I couldn't believe it!

First, the letter was approved on the day my son died. And second, it was approved for six figures to cover my medical bills. I was so in shock, I had to have my husband read it, and then my friend too, to ensure I had read it correctly! I was in tears to think that my son had initially encouraged me to submit the claim and that we received the approval on the day he took his last breath. It felt like he left me this gift before he left the earth.

To think, too, that God responded to my heart and prayers by relieving my husband from the financial pressure—glory, hallelujah! It's sweet moments like this that allowed me to see God at work, lifting this burden so we could pass through this valley with ease.

God supplied my needs when cancer came to rob my life and my finances. Now that I am on the other side, I trust He will do the same. I declare and believe my life after cancer will be peaceful because God, my Supplier, is taking care of me.

CIRCLES OF HONOR

A month after my reconstructive surgery, I hosted a dinner for five couple friends that stood by our side during the loss of our son. Whatever we needed, they were there. The guys held Bryan up, and the women gave me the support I needed. Whether it was texts, food, desserts, cards, gifts, prayer, or just sitting in the lobby of the hospital during our son's final days on this earth, they were there.

I spared no details to express our love. I hired a decorator to transform our dining room and a chef to prepare a delicious meal. Across each place setting was a gold place card that said "GRATEFUL." After dinner was served, I proceeded to thank each of them for being there for Bryan, myself, and my family during the loss of our son.

"However," I announced, "there was more we were going through at the time."

I shared with them I had been diagnosed with stage 4 breast cancer and then told them how well I was doing. A hush fell over the room, and some eyes filled with tears. I shared some details of the journey and why I chose to do it privately until I found my footing and strength. Even though they understood, they were pained to realize what I had gone through.

A few days later, it was time to honor my inner circle, the individuals who stood by me and held space for me while I journeyed through. I had heard God tell me to host this dinner and to call it the "Table of Honor." I knew this was a sign I was coming out of this season.

I contacted everyone to invite them to dinner at a steakhouse. After they were served a four-course meal, I went around the room to honor each of them individually. Through sobs, I told them how their support impacted my life. It was their support and holding space for me that allowed me to make it to that moment. I had put a gag order on them not to tell anyone about the cancer and treatment. Their support allowed me the room to trust God and not worry. It allowed me to grow and endure, no matter the cost. Their support kept me focused and connected to living, and I wanted them to know the impact they had on me.

Honoring them was like honoring God for

assembling this team around me during the most challenging season of my life. ∼⚘

WIDENING THE CIRCLE

I knew once I shared the story with those friends and honored my inner circle, next up would be sharing with the intercessory team. I thought it important to share with them privately before sharing it with the congregation because of the bond we shared as a team. I would have fractured their trust and created great pain and confusion if I had publicly shared that information without first informing them.

Even though I stepped away from this team for almost a year, I still participated in monthly calls, listened to the lessons, chimed in, and gave feedback. The team, in my absence, only knew I had been taking time away to care for my son and subsequently grieve his death. I held my story like a clam, sealing its shell until it was time for the precious pearl to be revealed to the outside world.

On that Saturday morning, I held a Zoom meeting and asked everyone to be on camera. I began by thanking them for their participation on the team and also thanking the interim leader, Minister Anthia. Then I shared a little about my son, his journey, and his passing. My eyes filled with tears, and I felt the grief in my body as if it had just happened. I was trying to find my way and the words to share my diagnosis and journey.

I looked at each person on camera as their eyes stared back at me. I mustered the courage to finally tell them that during the time my son was diagnosed for the second time, I too was diagnosed with metastatic breast cancer. With their mics on mute, I could see their eyes enlarge. I could guess they were fighting the emotions of confusion, shock, and fear. I told the story in detail and invited them to ask questions. No one responded. I knew they were too shocked to know what to ask. I left the door open to ask questions after they'd had a chance to process all I shared. By the end of the meeting, I could see some faces wiping tears. I closed out our meeting by letting them know how much I appreciated them and that I wanted them to know before I shared it with the congregation the next day.

That Sunday, I was so nervous. The time had come. It was time to face the congregation for the first time in more than five hundred days. To get my nerves under control and help organize my thoughts, due to the details and enormity of the story, I spoke with Varian to talk it out. She proposed that instead of telling the story, the presentation take place in an interview style. I would come up with seven questions that Pastor Riva could ask me, and I would share the story through the questions. This would give me the focus and freedom to share with some detail so the congregation could experience the ebbs and flows of my emotions, doubts, disappointments, as well as my faith and trust in God.

When I shared about the day I received the diagnosis of stage 4 breast cancer, you could hear the gasp in the room. Some images from the time I was in the hospital with the tubes hanging from me were projected on the LED wall behind me. The room was so quiet. Some heartfelt moments stirred up gratitude and brought tears to my eyes again, especially when I shared how my husband stood by my side the entire journey. I could see the congregation's reactions—eyes that filled with tears, shock, sadness, joy, and gladness to know I had emerged victorious from this battle. That day was filled with supportive well wishes, hugs, and gratitude by some. Others didn't know what to say; they needed time to process.

Sharing my story with everyone felt like relief—a final exhale and invitation to welcome others into my experience. My inner circle and I had held this close for so long. I felt released to take one more meaningful step back into the world.

A New Michele

"Nobody would know you are walking through cancer," my oncologist told me on one of my visits. Coming from a physician who sees numerous cancer patients on a daily basis, his feedback brought assurance and joy to my soul. His comment also reminded me of the times I would speak to Pastor Riva over the phone and she would say, "You sound so good. You don't sound like what you are walking through."

There were times I would send video messages to the church to update members on how I was doing after the loss of my son. When Pastor Riva reviewed them, she would say the same thing: "You don't look like what you've been through." This is a testament to God. He literally preserved me and gave me a treatment that protected me from hair loss, weight loss, less pain, skin discoloration, dizziness, and a host of other possible side effects.

I was thankful for His grace. But I knew I wasn't the same Michele. And it was now my turn to introduce the new Michele to myself. I'd been hidden for more than five hundred days. After walking through this battle, it was time to rebuild my confidence to see myself differently. It was time to reflect the new me to myself before showing up in the world. It was time to see myself differently and fully open and appreciate the beauty of my new wings.

I scheduled a photoshoot with a makeup artist, wardrobe consultant, and local photographer. This was my way of beginning to embody this new person within me. On the day of the photoshoot, I shared my story with my glam squad: Maura, my makeup artist; Natasha, my wardrobe consultant; and Edz, the photographer. They made me feel so beautiful and comfortable in front of the camera.

For so long, more than five hundred days, nearly everything in my life had felt like it was falling apart. The photoshoot helped me feel excited about the future. For the first time in a long time, I truly felt like everything was coming together. This butterfly was ready to take flight.

WORTH THE YES

Passion and pain have a purpose in our lives, even when we don't understand it. Passion (root word is *suffering*) is the willingness to go through challenges for something that is worth more than the present pain. You go through the pain because, in the end, you know it will be worth it. Your pain becomes purpose driven when you are in pursuit of something that matters more to you than the suffering. It makes enduring the suffering worth it.

Saying yes to God and yes to His leading through the darkest corridors of my life meant I also got to say yes to the honey moments and to seeing miracles sprinkled along my path. I have newfound relationships, connections, a cancer survivor ministry, and vision to support women in getting an early diagnosis.

Knowing the pain I endured in those five hundred days, would I take back my yes? Absolutely not! The yes opened me up to an abundant life God prepared and planned for me.

As we end this journey together and stand on the threshold of change, I invite you to raise your glass with me in celebration:

To faith in God, trusting in His guidance with every step we take in life.

To the unwavering faithfulness of God, a constant source of love and grace in our lives.

To seasons of faith, where belief paves the way for the unseen and the hoped-for.

To seasons of growth, as we evolve beyond our setbacks of yesterday, reaching toward the potential we possess.

To seasons of healing, soothing the scars of our past and embracing the peace and wholeness of the future.

To seasons of joy, where smiles become easier and laughter is our shared language.

To seasons of strength, forging an inner fortitude that defies life's challenges.

And to a season of new relationships, crafting bonds that enrich our lives with love, care, and support.

Here's to the season ahead; may it be richly blessed by His presence. Cheers!

Your Turn

Are you ready to say yes to seeing God's goodness in a fresh, new way and to trust Him more in your situation?

- How is your diagnosis changing your life? How are you adapting to this transformation? In what ways are you resisting changes?

- In what ways can you say yes to God in order to embrace the uncertainty that comes with transformation?

- What old habits or beliefs must you shed in order to allow for new growth?

- What internal work do you need to do before you can emerge anew?

- How can you remain patient and trust the process, even when progress seems slow or invisible?

A Closing Prayer

Father, thank You for this beautiful life that You grant us daily. Like the process of a caterpillar turning into a butterfly, we can be pressured and processed by our disappointments, adversities, lessons, and victories. Thank You for Your love, grace, and peace, which hold us together and guide us through the process. Teach us not to resist change but to embrace and endure it with Your guidance. Remind us that when we love You and are called by purpose, all things are working together for our good, according to Romans 8:28. We are strong in You and in the power of Your might. We are growing, transforming, and emerging powerfully into a new season. Prepare us for the next chapter of our lives as we emerge with outstretched wings to beautify the world with new ideas, insight, wisdom, passion, purpose, strength, and courage. In Jesus' name, amen!

A SALVATION INVITATION

S ALVATION, IN SIMPLE terms, is like being rescued from danger. Imagine you're stuck in a big, scary forest and someone shows you the way out. That's what salvation is like for your spirit.

As human beings, we are mind, body, and spirit. Salvation helps us feel safe from sinful things we've done and harmful things that may have been done to us. Salvation restores our relationship with God through accepting His Son, Jesus Christ, who through His death, burial, and resurrection saved us and has given us power over the evil one. This act of love was given to us through God as a result of His grace and mercy being extended to us.

Salvation gives us a fresh start in life. It erases mistakes of the past, gives us a clean slate, and teaches us how to become a better version of who we are and how to fulfill our purpose. No more living in doubt, worry, fear, and disappointment. We now have access to a renewed way of thinking.

Salvation gives us protection, grace, peace, freedom, wisdom, joy, and eternal life in Jesus Christ. Without salvation, we live life in fear, doubt, hopelessness, and emptiness, both in the earth and in hell. This never-ending journey of love and joy in Jesus Christ, through salvation, keeps us loving and honoring God for His love, grace, and mercy toward us.

Salvation is truly important because it helps us live better now, and it gives us great hope for an even brighter future. If you've not prayed the prayer of salvation and would like to, I invite you to pray this prayer with me:

> *Father, we thank You for choosing us before we even knew ourselves and for giving us the gift of love through Your Son, Jesus Christ. John 3:16 states that God so loved the world that He gave His only begotten Son, that whoever believes in Him will not perish but have everlasting life. We are thankful to know that through salvation, no matter what we go through, we have eternal life. Salvation gives us access to the grace, peace, joy, freedom, wisdom, power, and strength that comes through Jesus Christ. We are grateful that through salvation, we are never alone and that we always have the Savior in our hearts to lead, encourage, empower, and strengthen us through good times and times of disappointment.*
>
> *Today, we surrender everything and ask that You fill our hearts. We ask that You forgive us for any sins we have committed knowingly or unknowingly and any hurt that we may have caused to others. We accept Jesus Christ as our Savior; we believe in our hearts*

and confess with our mouths that through the death, burial, and resurrection of Jesus Christ, we have a new life. Come into our hearts and lead us to a life of love, joy, peace, freedom, wisdom, and success, now and forevermore. In Jesus' name, amen!

ABOUT THE AUTHOR

MICHELE DECAUL IS passionate about prayer and intercession, using her faith to empower, mentor, and coach women to become the best version of themselves as God intended. She is dedicated to ministering the Word of God to transform, empower, and heal lives. In her role as pastor of spiritual development, Michele focuses on training and developing leaders in mental, emotional, spiritual, and social aspects. Her goal is to equip them to navigate life, leadership, and relationships effectively.

In 2022, Michele faced personal challenges, laying her son to rest after his battle with a rare cancer. Just five months earlier, she was diagnosed with stage 4 breast cancer. Despite these trials, Michele emphasizes God's grace, strength, and healing in her life and family. Her journey through cancer, both as a caregiver and a patient, has deepened her relationship with God and taught her compassion for others facing similar challenges. Today, she aspires to be known as someone who has drawn closer to God and became His friend.

Michele is married to Bryan and is a proud mother of two daughters, Carrington and Kayla.

www.ingramcontent.com/pod-product-compliance
Lightning Source LLC
Chambersburg PA
CBHW071733120626
46550CB00002B/499